MW00462724

Science Warm-Ups

Authors: Linda Armstrong, Schyrlet Cameron, Carolyn Craig, Gary Raham, and Wendi Silvano

Editor: Mary Dieterich

Proofreaders: Lexi Albert and Margaret Brown

COPYRIGHT © 2016 Mark Twain Media, Inc.

ISBN 978-1-62223-638-1

Printing No. CD-404259

Mark Twain Media, Inc., Publishers
Distributed by Carson-Dellosa Publishing LLC

Table of Contents

Introduction

The *Science Warm-Ups* book provides students with a daily dose of science activities to get them warmed up for a day's lesson or to review what has already been learned. It is important for students to review and practice the skills they gain as they learn science concepts. Revisiting science concepts several days after they are first learned is a helpful way to reinforce those skills.

The short warm-up activities presented in this book provide teachers and parents with activities to help students practice and reinforce the skills they have already learned. One warm-up may be used to kick off a lesson, or an entire lesson can be built using related warm-ups from the book. The warm-ups can be used in any order to best meet your teaching needs.

Topics covered in *Science Warm-Ups* include general science and inquiry, life science, the human body, earth science, atmospheric science, space science, physical science, and science and technology. Many warm-ups focus on more basic one-step activities such as fill in the blank, matching, and true/false. Other warm-ups may involve more critical-thinking skills or be multi-step activities. Students may need to complete some of the activities on their own paper.

Each page may be copied and cut apart so that the individual sections can be used as quick warm-up activities to begin each day. The teacher may also give the student the entire page to keep in a folder or binder and complete as assigned. A transparency of the page may be made to project the activities for the whole class to see. A digital copy of the page can also be projected on the class whiteboard or projection device.

Extra copies of warm-ups may also be kept in the class learning center for students to complete when they have spare time for review or when the class has a few minutes before lunch or dismissal.

Science Warm-Ups supports the NSE standards for science. Also, the book has been correlated to current state, national, and provincial standards. Correlations for the book that apply to your location and needs may be found at www.carsondellosa.com.

Name: _____ Date: _____

General Science & Inquiry

#001. General Science 1

Fill in the missing letters.

1. small piece   p __ r __ __ c __ __

2. way of working   me __ __ o __

3. knowledge   __ c __ __ __ c __

4. grow larger   __ xp __ __ __

5. get smaller   c __ __ t __ a __ __

#002. General Science 2

Use the clues to unscramble these words.

1. an idea proven to be true:

   ctaf _____

2. a group of organized, related things:

   emysst _____

3. something that makes something else

   happen: seuca _____

4. something that has been made to

   happen: ctffee _____

#003. General Science 3

Draw lines to match the words with their meanings.

1. **concept**   write down or save

2. **observe**   find similarities

3. **compare**   find differences

4. **contrast**   idea

5. **record**   watch

#004. General Science 4

Fill in the blank with the correct word from the box.

> repeat   experiment   hypothesis
> identify   theory

1. a logical, testable explanation
   _____

2. an explanation made as a starting place
   for discussion _____

3. a controlled test made to gain knowledge
   _____

4. to define or name something
   _____

5. to do or say again _____

Name: _____   Date: _____

General Science & Inquiry

#005. General Science 5

Draw lines to match words with meanings.

1. **state**   basic

2. **force**   move

3. **fundamental**   temporary form

4. **flow**   part

5. **unit**   energy

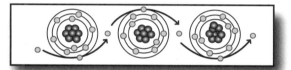

#006. General Science 6

Read each clue. Unscramble the word.

1. to research:
   iesntigatev _____

2. a skilled way of working:
   uechteqni _____

3. to define size, weight, or temperature:
   sureame _____

4. a state of being, such as sickness or health:
   itioncodn _____

5. something that has mass and occupies space:
   ansustceb _____

#007. General Science 7

Write T for true or F for false.

_____ 1. A **category** is a kind of panther.

_____ 2. The word **rapid** means very fast.

_____ 3. To **combine** means to take apart.

_____ 4. If something is **toxic**, it is poisonous.

_____ 5. To **penetrate** means to measure.

#008. General Science 8

Write the word from the box that matches each clue.

| volume | mass | weight |
| density | speed | |

1. mass per measured unit of an object; compactness _____

2. rate of motion; fast or slow
   _____

3. amount of matter an object contains
   _____

4. amount of space an object occupies
   _____

5. heaviness or lightness of an object
   _____

Name: _____   Date: _____

General Science & Inquiry

#009. General Science 9

Circle True or False for each statement.

1. When a planet *rotates*, it turns on its axis.
   True   False

2. A *component* is a kind of fish.
   True   False

3. To *alternate* means to go back and forth.
   True   False

4. A *cycle* is something that happens once and stops.
   True   False

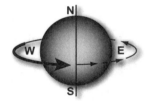

#010. General Science 10

Draw lines to match each term to its meaning.

1. **kilogram**   a hundredth of a meter

2. **gram**   basic metric unit of weight

3. **milligram**   a thousandth of a meter

4. **millimeter**   a thousandth of a gram

5. **centimeter**   a thousand grams

#011. General Science 11

Fill in the missing letters.

1. assigned duty   f __ __ ct __ __ n

2. reasoning from something known

   __ n __ __ r __ __ __ e

3. inquire or examine

   in __ __ __ ti __ a __ e

4. meters and kilograms

   m __ __ __ __ c measurements

5. description used for discussion and

   investigation   m __ d __ l

#012. General Science 12

Write the word from the box that best completes each sentence.

thriving	transfer	variables
volume	Venn diagram	

1. He drew a _____ to show which animals ate both insects and seeds.

2. The _____ of the tank was 38 cubic meters.

3. The meadow was a _____ community of plants and animals.

4. Temperature, rainfall, and wind direction were important _____.

5. Genes _____ information from one generation to the next.

Name: _____ Date: _____

General Science & Inquiry

#013. General Science 13

Circle the word that best fits each clue.

1. order: segment   sequence

2. outcome: cause   result

3. exact: precise   estimate

4. part: segment   system

5. identify: assume   name

#014. General Science 14

Circle T for true or F for false.

T F **1.** *Efficiency* means the best use of energy.

T F **2.** To *assume* means to prove.

T F **3.** To *extend* means to stretch out.

T F **4.** To *belong* means to be left out.

T F **5.** To *conclude* means to observe.

#015. General Science 15

Write the word that best completes each sentence.

interference   equilibrium   imbalance

1. Snowfall and melting reached an

_____, and the glacier

stopped growing.

2. An _____ in

squirrel birth and death rates

caused overpopulation.

#016. General Science 16

Draw a line to connect the word with its definition.

1. **collide**   does not change

2. **absolute**   depends upon changing

conditions

3. **principles**   run into each other

4. **relative**   fundamental rules or laws

Name: _____ Date: _____

General Science & Inquiry

#017. General Science 17

Fill in the missing letters.

1. a well-established observation about nature

   __ c __ e __ ti __ __ c   l __ __

2. a preliminary idea about how something in nature works

   s __ __ __ n __ i __ ic   m __ d __ l

3. a testable model based on repeatable experimental evidence

   s __ ien __ __ __ ic   __ h __ o __ y

4. use of observation and experimentation to develop and test ideas

   s __ i __ n __ __ __ ic   m __ __ __ od

#018. General Science 18

Circle T for true or F for false.

T F 1. When water changes to ice, it is a reversible process.

T F 2. Scientists never evaluate the results of their experiments.

T F 3. If there is more food today, the quality of the food has increased.

T F 4. If there is more pollution, the quantity of pollution has increased.

T F 5. It is only necessary to perform an experiment once to make a valid conclusion.

#019. General Science 19

Use the clue to unscramble each word.

1. how often something happens:

   uenfrcyeq _____

2. how things depend on each other:

   onsitterreinlahip _____

3. likely:

   babperol _____

4. move away:

   drecee _____

5. move toward:

   vacenad _____

#020. General Science 20

Draw a line to match each word with the best clue.

1. **replicate**   importance

2. **submerge**   nonliving

3. **boundary**   sink

4. **inorganic**   copy

5. **significance**   limit

Name: _____ Date: _____

General Science & Inquiry

#021. Doing Stuff With Matter & Energy 1

All **mass** resists being moved. This property is called **inertia**.

Place an index card on top of a glass. Place a penny on the card. Remove the card quickly by yanking on it with two fingers so that the penny drops into the glass.

1. Explain how this demonstrates inertia.

   _____
   _____
   _____

2. If you move the card slowly (with the coin on top of it), does the coin move with the card? _____

3. What force keeps the coin from sliding off?

   _____

#022. Doing Stuff With Matter & Energy 2

On your own paper, design a plan for determining how you could tell if each of the following substances is an **element**, **compound**, **heterogeneous mixture**, or **solution**.

1. salt water

2. cracker

3. baking powder

4. penny

5. instant oatmeal

#023. Doing Stuff With Matter & Energy 3

Fill a small, clear jar half full of water. Mark the water level on the side of the jar with a wax pencil or marker. Take a small watertight plastic container and fill it with sand. Seal the lid and place the container in the jar of water. You may want to put tape around the lid to make sure it is watertight. Mark the new water level on the side of the jar. Repeat the procedure after replacing the sand with modeling clay.

1. Does the amount of water displaced depend on the **mass** or **volume** of the film container?

   _____

2. On your own paper, tell how you could measure the actual volume of a solid using this method.

#024. Doing Stuff With Matter & Energy 4

One of the most reactive groups of nonmetals in the Periodic Table of the Elements is the **halogens** (Family 17), which includes **fluorine**, **chlorine**, **bromine**, and **iodine**. Gather four labels of household products or cleaners, or use labels provided by your teacher. On your own paper, list the names of the products and the halogens used in each one.

Which products seem to require the most care to use?

_____

_____

_____

Name: _____ Date: _____

General Science & Inquiry

#025. Doing Stuff With Living Things: Day 1

Make a creepy crawler observatory.

Materials:
1 piece of clear acetate approximately 5.5″ x 17″
1 piece of cardboard 8.5″ x 11″
1 piece of picture glass or Plexiglas 8″ x 10″

Directions: Tape a piece of graph paper to one side of the cardboard or rule it with a grid of lines 1 cm apart. Bend the acetate to form a ring and either tape or staple the ends together. The complete observatory will look like the diagram at the right.

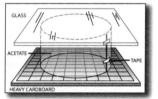

#026. Doing Stuff With Living Things: Day 2

Make a pit trap to get live subjects for your creepy crawler observatory.

Materials: a can with one end removed or a wide-mouthed jar, a piece of cardboard big enough to cover the can, 4 small pebbles, and 1 larger rock.

Directions: Bury the can in the ground so that the top is even with ground level. Put pebbles around the can so that when the cardboard is placed on top, there is a gap of $\frac{1}{4}$″ or $\frac{1}{2}$″ between the cardboard and ground. Hold the cardboard in place with a larger rock.

#027. Doing Stuff With Living Things: Day 3

Collect creepy crawlers from a pit trap or other sources. Separate the animals into their own containers. Create an observation sheet with the following headers: **Date**, **Behavior Observed**, **Drawing**, and **Animal Identity.**

Place one animal in the observatory at a time. Record the date. Sketch the animal. Record its appearance and behavior. Make a sketch of the animal (top and bottom). Note any colors.

#028. Doing Stuff With Living Things: Day 4

Find two creepy crawlers of the same kind and put them in the observatory. Record the date. Under "Behavior Observed" record how they interact with each other.

Jumping spiders make good subjects. They are "nervous" spiders with two big eyes in front and six smaller eyes to the side. They tend to be hairy with bright markings. They raise their forelegs when meeting other jumping spiders. Males do zigzag dances to impress females.

Name: _____ Date: _____

General Science & Inquiry

#029. Doing Stuff With Ecosystems & Habitats: Day 1

Create a set of five microbial gardens in five resealable plastic bags, which you will watch over the next four days.

1. Place some cut-up grapes, slightly crushed in bag #1.
2. Place a few dried beans and $\frac{1}{2}$ cup water in bag #2.
3. Place a few leaves of lettuce and water in bag #3.
4. Place a piece of stale bread, slightly moistened, in bag #4.
5. Place cottage cheese in bag #5.
6. Seal the bags and place somewhere out of direct sunlight.

#030. Doing Stuff With Ecosystems & Habitats: Day 2

Create a one-page chart with the following headers: **Date**, **Appearance**, **Appearance (magnified)**, and **Organism**.

On your chart, record today's date and describe the appearance of the items in each bag. Each time you observe the bags, look at them with the naked eye and also with a magnifying glass. Leave the Organism column blank for now.

#031. Doing Stuff With Ecosystems & Habitats: Day 3

On your chart, record today's date and describe the appearance of the items in each bag.

If any bag has filled with gas, have your teacher bleed some air out of the bag.

Answer these questions on your own paper.

1. What gases might be created in these "gardens"?
2. What kind of microorganisms might you expect to find in each bag?
3. What differences are you noting in what grows in each bag?

#032. Doing Stuff With Ecosystems & Habitats: Day 4

On your chart, record and observe as before. Draw sketches if necessary, using colored pencils. **Bacterial colonies** tend to be moist and shiny looking. **Fungi** reproduce with spores held on stalks and may look fuzzy. Make a list of the number of different microorganisms you see in each bag, and under the heading Organism, indicate whether you think it is a fungus or a bacterium.

On your own paper, explain how you could design a way to see if temperature affected the growth of "microbial gardens."

Name: _____ Date: _____

General Science & Inquiry

#033. Doing Stuff With Astronomy & Space Science 1

Planets travel in elliptical orbits around the sun, with the sun located at one of the **foci** of the **ellipse**.

Create an ellipse by placing two pushpins in a piece of thick cardboard. Take a length of string, tie the ends together, and loop it around the pushpins. With a pencil, point side down, stretch the string loop to its limits so that it forms a triangle. Maintaining outward pressure with the pencil, rotate it around the pushpins, letting the pencil lead create an arc. When you reach the starting point, you have created an ellipse—a kind of squashed circle. Experiment with changing the distance between foci and the length of the string.

#034. Doing Stuff With Astronomy & Space Science 2

You can't look directly at the sun without damaging your eyes, but you can view the sun after making a **camera obscura** with a cardboard box, some tape, a box cutter, a needle, and piece of white paper. (See picture below.)

Point the needle hole toward the sun, stick your head in the side hole, and the sun will be projected onto the white paper. This is great for seeing eclipses, too!

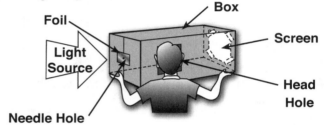

#035. Doing Stuff With Astronomy & Space Science 3

Weigh too much? You just need to visit the right planet. Your **weight** depends on the **mass** of the planet on which you live. If Earth's **gravity** is given a value of 1, the other planets would be as follows: Mercury: 0.38; Venus: 0.91; Mars: 0.38; Jupiter 2.53; Saturn: 1.07; Uranus: 0.91; Neptune: 1.16.

1. On which planets would you weigh less than on Earth?

   _____

   _____

   _____

2. If you weigh 100 pounds on Earth, on which planet would you weigh 116 pounds?

   _____

#036. Doing Stuff With Astronomy & Space Science 4

Moon Match: Draw a line between the planets on the left and their moons on the right.

1. Mars   **Io**

                      Titan

2. Jupiter   **Mimas**

                      Miranda

3. Saturn   **Europa**

                      Phobos

4. Uranus   **Enceladus**

                      Callisto

Name: _____ Date: _____

General Science & Inquiry

#037. Doing Stuff With Earth Materials 1

Make a kit for determining the hardness of various rocks and minerals based on the **Mohs hardness scale**. Your kit should include a copper penny (3.5); a piece of glass (5); and a steel file or nail (6.5). Your fingernail has a hardness of 2.5. An object can scratch anything with the same hardness or softer (lower number). These items can be kept in a resealable plastic bag.

Mohs Hardness Scale

Talc 1	Gypsum 2
Calcite 3	Fluorite 4
Apatite 5	Orthoclase 6
Quartz 7	Topaz 8
Corundum 9	Diamond 10

#038. Doing Stuff With Earth Materials 2

Create a series of cards for each rock and mineral that you collect. Put the following headers on 3″ x 5″ index cards: Date collected; Formation (if known); Location; Catalog #. The Catalog # should be recorded in a separate notebook. One possible system is to use your initials followed by a collection number.

#039. Doing Stuff With Earth Materials 3

Grow a crystal. Mix a hot, saturated solution of alum or copper sulfate in a beaker. Tie one end of a thread to the middle of a pencil, and place the pencil across the beaker so that the thread dangles  into the solution. Let the solution cool slowly. Save the biggest crystal on the thread and remove the rest. Reheat the solution and repeat the process as many times as necessary to get a large crystal. The same process happens in nature.

#040. Doing Stuff With Earth Materials 4

Create your own **sedimentary rock**.

Materials: Get a clear plastic container, a bag of plaster of Paris, and an assortment of earth materials like sand, gravel, pebbles, and shells.

Directions: Put an inch of plaster of Paris in the bottom of the container. Add an inch of earth material, then another layer of plaster. Add shells to simulate fossils. When the container is full, add as much water as the container will hold and let it sit overnight.

How does actual rock formation differ? How is it similar? _____

_____

_____

Name: _____ Date: _____

General Science & Inquiry

#041. Doing Stuff With Ancient Life 1

What things from our time will fossilize to become "future fossils"?

Materials: modeling clay and five objects or parts of objects from your classroom

Directions: Divide the modeling clay into five pieces. Press each of the five objects into a piece of clay to make a mold or impression. Exchange your molds with those of someone else and try to guess what their objects were.

What are some of the problems in interpreting

fossils? _____

_____

_____

_____

#042. Doing Stuff With Ancient Life 2

1. Take 100 pennies and place them heads up in 10 rows of 10. Pretend these coins represent atoms of the radioactive element **potassium-40** (K^{40}).

2. In 1.3 billion years, half of a sample of K^{40} will change to **argon-40** (Ar^{40}). Turn over half the rows of pennies, making them tails up (which represents Ar^{40}). 1.3 billion years is the **half-life** of K^{40}.

3. In another 1.3 billion years, half of the K^{40} left will change to Ar^{40}. Flip over 25 more pennies.

By measuring the ratio of radioactive elements and their decay products, scientists can measure the age of **fossils** imbedded in or near those rocks.

#043. Doing Stuff With Ancient Life 3

Pill bugs or "roly-poly" bugs are tiny land crustaceans that can roll up into a ball when touched. **Trilobites** were shelled animals that lived on ocean bottoms many years ago. Some of them could also roll up (see picture). List some reasons why this behavior might have been important for each animal.

_____

_____

_____

_____

_____

_____

#044. Doing Stuff With Ancient Life 4

Dinosaurs didn't all live at the same time. Early dinosaurs arose in the Triassic period of the Mesozoic Era. Dinosaurs flourished during the Jurassic period of the same era, then died out at the end of the Cretaceous period. Match each dinosaur with its proper time period.

A. Cretaceous B. Jurassic C. Triassic

____ 1. Coelophysis

____ 2. Tyrannosaurus rex

____ 3. Parasaurolophus

____ 4. Stegosaurus

____ 5. Brachiosaurus

____ 6. Triceratops

____ 7. Allosaurus

Name: _____ Date: _____

Life Science

#045. Life Science 1

Unscramble each word.

1. study of living things in the places they live: **ceyoolg** _____
2. group of living things: **mmncotiuy** _____
3. all land, sea, and air containing living things: **eerhpoibs** _____
4. air, sea, or land around a living thing: **eeonnnirmtv** _____
5. change that helps a living thing fit its surroundings: **onaaatpdti** _____

#046. Life Science 2

Fill in the missing letters.

1. sorting items into groups
   cl __ __ __ ifi __ __ t __ __ n
2. things that are not alive
   __ __ __ l __ __ __ __ g
3. scientific term for things that are alive
   o __ g __ n __ __ __ s
4. specific types of living things
   s __ __ c __ __ s

#047. Life Science 3

Fill in the blanks with one of these words.

herbivores   carnivores   omnivores

1. Animals that eat only meat are _____.
2. Animals that eat only plants are _____.
3. Animals that eat meat and plants are _____.

#048. Life Science 4

Circle T for true or F for false.

T F 1. A food web includes **producers**, **consumers**, and **decomposers**.

T F 2. A producer breaks down dead plants and animals.

T F 3. A producer changes light energy to food energy.

T F 4. Consumers eat producers.

T F 5. A **food web** is a special spider web.

Name: _____   Date: _____

Life Science

#049. Life Science 5

Draw lines to match words to clues.

1. **mammal**   is an invertebrate

2. **reptile**   lives part of life on land and part in water

3. **amphibian**   has fur or hair

4. **bird**   has scales

5. **mollusk**   has feathers

#050. Life Science 6

Circle the best example for each term.

1. **offspring**:   calf   rock   soil

2. **trait**:   cat   ocean   eye color

3. **behavior**:   size   diving   caves

4. **habitat**:   chasing   howling   forest

5. **juvenile**:   desert   kitten   markings

#051. Life Science 7

Fill in the blank with the letter of the correct word.

A. life cycle	**B. maturity**
C. inheritance	**D. lifespan**

1. A certain beak, size, and coloring are a bird's ___.

2. The tadpole phase is part of a frog's ___.

3. The length of an animal's life is its ___.

4. A term for an animal's adulthood is ___.

#052. Life Science 8

Draw lines to match terms and definitions

1. **membrane**   control center of a cell

2. **cytoplasm**   contents of a cell, except the nucleus

3. **cell**   tiny structures with special tasks in the cell

4. **organelles**   a basic unit of life

5. **nucleus**   a thin wall or layer

Name: _____ Date: _____

Life Science

#053. Life Science 9

Circle T for true or F for false.

T F **1.** **Diversity** means that only one type of animal lives an in area.

T F **2.** **Genes** carry the code of heredity.

T F **3.** Some animals survive the winter by **hibernating**.

T F **4.** **Migration** is a way for animals to hide from enemies.

T F **5.** A **larva** is an adult insect.

#054. Life Science 10

Circle the word that fits each meaning.

1. coloration that hides an animal:

   diversity   camouflage   prey

2. an animal that is hunted:

   transpiration   camouflage   prey

3. the act of imitating or copying:

   mimicry   parasitism   osmosis

4. disappearing from the earth:

   osmosis   extinction   transpiration

5. an animal that hunts:

   predator   gene   diversity

#055. Life Science 11

Circle the word or words in each line that are parts of a tree.

1. branch   crown

2. compost   bulb

3. cone   humus

4. needle   limb

#056. Life Science 12

Write the letter of the best word on each line.

> **A. seeds   B. germinate   C. embryo**
> **D. propagation   E. runners**

Our class is studying plant (**1**) _____. We planted some (**2**) _____. Each seed contained a baby plant, or (**3**) _____. It took a week for the seeds to (**4**) _____. We learned that plants do not always grow from seeds. Some grow from (**5**) _____.

Name: _____ Date: _____

Life Science

#057. Life Science 13

Circle the term that fits the clue.

1. creating fuel from light:

    photosynthesis   chlorophyll

2. location of **chlorophyll**:

    root   leaf   trunk

3. gas created through **photosynthesis**:

    oxygen   hydrogen

4. green substance in leaves:

    carbon dioxide   chlorophyll

5. gas used in photosynthesis:

    carbon dioxide   oxygen

#058. Life Science 14

Circle T for true or F for false.

T   F   **1.** **Soil** is a combination of crumbled rock, humus, air, and water.

T   F   **2.** **Humus** is a kind of dip eaten as a snack.

T   F   **3.** **Compost** can be used to enrich soils.

T   F   **4.** **Peat** usually forms in swamps or bogs.

#059. Life Science 15

Write the term from the box that best fits each clue.

| pistil | petal | stigma |
| pollen | ovary | |

1. base of the pistil, where seeds develop

    _____

2. sticky tip of the style, receives pollen

    _____

3. fertilizes ovules to create seeds

    _____

4. often colorful, helps to attract insects

    _____

5. the ovary, style, and stigma of a flower

    _____

#060. Life Science 16

Write the word that best fits each clue.

| biome | physical | exchange |
| distribution | | utility |

1. trade: _____

2. usefulness: _____

3. A grassland is an example of a _____.

4. A rock cracking is an example of a _____ change.

5. spread: _____

Name: _____ Date: _____

Life Science

#061. Life Science 17

Circle the term that best fits each clue.

1. related to breathing:

   digestion   respiration   excretion

2. related to breaking down food:

   digestion   respiration   excretion

3. waste disposal:

   digestion   respiration   excretion

4. transport of materials:

   digestion   circulation   regulation

5. many-celled:

   pituitary   temporal   multicellular

#062. Life Science 18

Circle T for true or F for false.

T F **1.** **Red blood cells** are specialized to perform certain jobs.

T F **2.** **Microorganisms** live only on microscope lenses.

T F **3.** **Pollination** is often performed by insects.

T F **4.** Gravity, wind, and animal activities help with **seed dispersal**.

#063. Life Science 19

Write the letter of the best word on each line.

A. nitrogen   B. osmosis   C. niche
D. nitrogen cycle

1. _____ is the movement of a fluid through a membrane.

2. A _____ is an organism's special place in an ecosystem.

3. Most of the gas in the atmosphere is _____.

4. As part of the _____, bacteria change a gas to a form plants can use.

#064. Life Science 20

Draw a line to match each term to the best clue.

1. **gills**   outside

2. **mates**   inside

3. **internal**   reaction

4. **external**   goose and gander

5. **response**   respiratory organ of a fish

Name: _____ Date: _____

Life Science

#065. Understanding Living Things 1

Potato plants take carbon dioxide from the air and, with the help of energy from sunlight, turn it into starchy  roots that people dig up and eat. Potatoes are then either eaten or rot away. This describes the typical roles of green plants, animals, and fungi: they are **producers**, **consumers**, and **decomposers**.

1. The "job" of a potato plant in nature is to

   be a _____.

2. Potatoes use the energy of sunlight to

   change carbon dioxide into _____.

#066. Understanding Living Things 2

A mushroom cap can release up to 600,000 **spores** per minute from its **gills** for as long as four days. You can see what these spores look like by removing a mushroom's cap and placing it, gill side down, on a piece of paper overnight. When you remove the cap, the fallen spores will have made a **spore print** on the paper.

1. A spore print is composed of many

   hundreds of thousands of _____.

2. To make a print, you have to place a

   mushroom's cap _____ side down

   on a piece of paper.

#067. Understanding Living Things 3

Snow fleas are primitive insects no longer than a sharpened pencil lead. Most are smaller. They are rarely seen except in winter when their population size increases. They then blunder up through holes in the snow from their soil and leaf litter homes.

1. Snow fleas live in _____ and

   _____ _____.

2. Most snow fleas are smaller than a

   _____ _____

   _____.

#068. Understanding Living Things 4

Jumping spiders are hairy spiders with two large eyes for hunting prey and six smaller eyes for detecting motion. They "talk" with other jumping spiders by waving their two front legs and showing colorful body markings.

1. Jumping spiders have a total of _____

   eyes.

2. Jumping spiders don't talk with words but

   communicate to each other by waving

   their _____

   and showing _____

   _____.

Name: _____   Date: _____

Life Science

#069. Figuring Out Living Things 1

Draw a line connecting the animal to the characteristic that correctly describes it.

1. **lobster**   marsupial mammal

2. **ant**   warm-blooded flyer

3. **sparrow**   has backbone, breathes through skin

4. **kangaroo**   has 3-part body, 6 legs

5. **frog**   a kind of crustacean

#070. Figuring Out Living Things 2

Draw a line connecting the plant to the characteristic that correctly describes it.

1. **daisy**   spores found beneath leaves

2. **moss**   has seeds in cones

3. **lichen**   attracts pollinators with flowers

4. **fern**   spores on stalks

5. **pine tree**   combination of algae and fungus

#071. Figuring Out Living Things 3

Living things are grouped into five large kingdoms: **plants**, **animals**, **fungi**, **protista**, and **bacteria**. Write the correct kingdom next to each organism.

1. spinach   _____

2. amoeba   _____

3. tick   _____

4. salmonella   _____

5. bread mold   _____

#072. Figuring Out Living Things 4

Female **dragonflies** usually search for a nice quiet pond where they can swoop down and lay their eggs just below the water's surface.

Why do you think dragonflies sometimes bang into the hoods of shiny cars on bright, sunny days?

_____

_____

_____

_____

_____

_____

Name: _____ Date: _____

Life Science

#073. Asking About Ecosystems & Habitats 1

Biodiversity is a word that refers to how varied the mixture of living things is in a community. Use a search engine like <u>yahoo.com</u> or <u>google.com</u> and search for the term "biodiversity."

1. Find the names of three scientists who have written about biodiversity.

   _____

   _____

2. List at least one question scientists are trying to answer about biodiversity.

   _____

   _____

   _____

#074. Asking About Ecosystems & Habitats 2

Below are the answers to three questions. Write the question asked for each answer.

1. Answer: **mayfly nymph**, **water boatman**, **stone-fly nymph**

   _____

   _____

2. Answer: **food webs**

   _____

   _____

3. Answer: **succession**

   _____

   _____

#075. Asking About Ecosystems & Habitats 3

Place the letter of the correct answer on the line next to the question.

> A. **second-order consumers**
> B. **decomposers**
> C. **producers**
> D. **first-order consumers**

1. What makes its own food supply? _____

2. What eats plants? _____

3. What eats plant eaters? _____

4. What breaks down dead bodies? _____

#076. Asking About Ecosystems & Habitats 4

A new manufacturing plant moves into your community and dumps some of its waste in a nearby river. List three questions you would want the manufacturers to answer for you.

1. _____

   _____

2. _____

   _____

3. _____

   _____

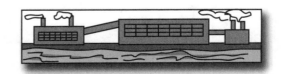

Name: _____ Date: _____

Life Science

#077. Understanding Ecosystems & Habitats 1

If a **milkweed** plant could run an advertisement in the newspaper, it might look like this: HELP WANTED: to take pollen to my relatives. Will exchange for really good food. Call 1-800-MLK-WEED.

1. True or False? Milkweed plants typically run ads in the newspaper. _____

2. Milkweed plants give other creatures _____ in order to transfer their _____ to other milkweed plants.

#078. Understanding Ecosystems & Habitats 2

When **sea otters** near California were killed for their fur, the number of **sea urchins**, the otters' favorite food, increased greatly. The sea urchins ate all the kelp "forests." The fish and other creatures dependent on the kelp died, destroying the entire ecosystem.

1. True or False? The loss of sea otters near California had a temporary effect on fish populations in the kelp forests. _____

2. Without sea otters to control their numbers, _____ _____ ate nearly all the kelp in the sea off the coast of California.

#079. Understanding Ecosystems & Habitats 3

The **Colorado potato beetle**, when first discovered in 1823, ate and laid its eggs on a weed called buffalo bur. When potatoes, a plant in the same family as the weed, were planted by farmers in the 1880s, the beetles began eating them and became a pest.

1. True or False? Certain insects can switch the plants they normally feed on. _____

2. Potatoes and buffalo bur are plants in the same _____.

#080. Understanding Ecosystems & Habitats 4

Populations of animals increase very quickly when food is plentiful, there is room to grow, and not many predators. Population numbers level off as food and space decrease and eventually "crash" to very low numbers.

1. True or False? Animal populations vary randomly with the amount of food available. _____

2. Three limits to population growth are _____, _____, and _____.

Name: _____ Date: _____

Life Science

#081. Figuring Out Ecosystems & Habitats 1

Parasitic worms that infect salamanders cause those animals to be born with deformed legs when the worms form cysts near where baby salamanders will grow legs. Scientists also found that if they put sterile glass beads in the same place, the legs would also be deformed. This experiment shows that (circle one):

a. cysts make chemicals that cause leg deformities.

b. any object placed near legs forming in salamanders may cause deformities.

c. you shouldn't throw glass beads in lakes and ponds.

d. glass beads can cause infections.

#082. Figuring Out Ecosystems & Habitats 2

Many plants create brightly colored flowers. Some have flowers that look like insects. Others have flowers that smell like feces or rotting flesh. Some flowers have markings called nectar guides that point toward the center of the flower.

What do all these flowering plants have in common?

_____

_____

_____

_____

#083. Figuring Out Ecosystems & Habitats 3

Insects attacked sage plants in large numbers. Several minutes later, downwind, a group of tobacco plants began producing a chemical that repelled the same insects.

How do you think the tobacco plants "learned" about the pest insects?

_____

_____

_____

_____

#084. Figuring Out Ecosystems & Habitats 4

Spittlebugs are small insects that make "spit bubbles" using special abdominal glands. The insects let the spit build up all around them. It eventually gets hard enough that rain won't even wash it away.

Make a list of the ways this spit might be useful for the bug. How could you test your ideas?

_____

_____

_____

_____

Name: _____   Date: _____

Human Body

#085. Human Body 1

Fill in the missing letters.

1. a repeated series of events c __ c __ e

2. tissues grouped together to perform a function o __ __ __ n

3. a group of similar cells acting together to perform a function t __ s __ u __

4. organs grouped together to perform a function o __ g __ __ s __ __ t __ m

Liver

#086. Human Body 2

Using the clue, unscramble each word or phrase.

1. brain and spinal cord:
   enalctr vusnero steysm
   _____

2. center for thought and control of body functions:
   nrbai _____

3. special cells that carry information:
   snveer _____

4. cord that carries information from the brain to body:
   alsinp rcod _____

5. something that causes a response:
   ultimsus _____

#087. Human Body 3

Write the letter of the correct term on each line.

> **A. circulatory system**   **B. heart**
> **C. cardiac**   **D. chambers**
> **E. cardiac muscle**

The word (**1**) _____ refers to a special pump, the (**2**) _____. It is an important part of the (**3**) _____. It is made from (**4**) _____, and it has four sections, or (**5**) _____.

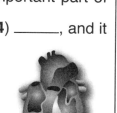

#088. Human Body 4

Using the clues, unscramble each term.

1. Breaks down food for use by cells in the body:
   evegtisdi _____ system

2. Pouch-like organ where food is broken down:
   macohst _____

3. Tube-like organ where food is digested and absorbed:
   nestestini _____

4. Tube from the mouth to the stomach:
   ehagussop _____

5. Releases substances that control the use of fuels from food:
   vrlie _____

Name: _____ Date: _____

Human Body

#089. Human Body 5

Write the letter of the correct term on each line.

> **A. spine**   **B. skeletal system**
> **C. marrow**   **D. bones**

The (1) _____ supports the body. It consists of the skull, (2) _____, and the (3) _____. Tissues inside the bones, in the (4) _____ produce blood cells. This system also includes joints and connective tissue.

#090. Human Body 6

Circle the part of the body where each can be found.

1.	**femur**:	hips	arms	legs
2.	**pelvis**:	hips	arms	legs
3.	**patella**:	knee	elbow	heel
4.	**rib**:	chest	hips	skull
5.	**sternum**:	chest	knee	elbow

#091. Human Body 7

Write the letter of the correct term on each line.

> **A. bronchial tubes**   **B. oxygen**
> **C. lungs**   **D. respiratory system**
> **E. diaphragm**

The (1) _____ brings fresh (2) _____ into the body and carries away carbon dioxide. Powerful muscles in the (3) _____ expand the chest cavity to pull air into the (4) _____ through the (5) _____.

#092. Human Body 8

Circle the correct term.

1. relating to the eye:

   optic   auditory   dental

2. relating to hearing:

   optic   auditory   dental

3. part of the tooth:

   retina   saliva   dentin

4. fluid in the mouth:

   retina   saliva   dentin

5. part of the eye:

   retina   saliva   dentin

Name: _____   Date: _____

Human Body

#093. Human Body 9

Fill in the missing letters.

1. This type of organ produces chemicals the body needs.

   g __ __ __ d

2. This gland produces hormones.

   e __ __ oc __ __ n __

3. These glands release adrenaline.

   a __ __ e __ __ l

4. This gland produces insulin and digestive juices.   p __ __ c __ __ __ s

#094. Human Body 10

Draw a line to connect each clue to the correct term

1. system that moves waste out of the body   **urethra**

2. one of two organs that remove waste from blood   **bladder**

3. organ where urine is stored   **excretory**

4. organ that removes waste through perspiration   **kidney**

5. tube connecting bladder to the outside of the body   **skin**

#095. Human Body 11

Circle T for true or F for false.

T F 1. The **biceps** is found in the leg.

T F 2. The **triceps** is found in the arm.

T F 3. The **muscular system** breaks down food for the body.

T F 4. When muscles relax, they get thicker and shorter.

T F 5. When muscles contract, they get thicker and shorter.

#096. Human Body 12

Write the letter of the best term on each line.

A. spleen   B. nodes   C. lymph
D. lymphatic system

The job of the (**1**) _____ is to fight infection and maintain the body's fluid balance. It carries a fluid called (**2**) _____ from the tissues into the bloodstream. The (**3**) _____ produces cells that help to fight disease. Lymph (**4**) _____ help to filter bacteria and waste from the lymph fluid.

Name: _____ Date: _____

Human Body

#097. Human Body 13

Circle T for true or F for false.

T F **1.** **Starch** is found in potatoes and rice.

T F **2.** All **fiber** is easy to digest.

T F **3.** **Proteins** are **macronutrients**.

T F **4.** **Vitamins** are **micronutrients**.

T F **5.** **Fats** are unnecessary in a healthy diet.

#098. Human Body 14

Unscramble each term.

1. the hard outer layer of the tooth:

eeamln _____

2. tissue around the pulp inside the tooth:

etdinn _____

3. part of the tooth below the gum:

orot _____

4. part of the tooth above the gum line:

rnocw _____

5. firm tissues around your teeth:

musg _____

#099. Human Body 15

Unscramble each term.

1. basic unit of heredity: **ngee** _____

2. thread-like part of a cell that contains genes:

roommosche _____

3. a molecule that contains coded hereditary information: **NDA** _____

4. smallest particle of a particular compound or element: **leulecmo** _____

5. traits passed from one generation to the next: **heyditer** _____

#100. Human Body 16

Write the letter of the best term on each line.

> **A. infectious**   **B. immune system**
> **C. lymphocytes**   **D. barriers**

The (**1**) _____ defends the body against (**2**) _____ diseases. Many (**3**) _____ guard the body, including the skin. (**4**) _____ in the bloodstream attack invaders.

Name: _____ Date: _____

Human Body

#101. Human Body 17

Unscramble each term.

1. good physical condition:

   esitfns _____

2. ease of movement:

   liibifltyxe _____

3. in the presence of oxygen:

   erabico _____

4. lasting power, stamina:

   edurennca _____

#102. Human Body 18

Write the letter of the best term on each line.

> **A. sound waves**   **B. vibrate**
> **C. eardrum**   **D. impulses**
> **E. auditory canal**

When (**1**) _____ enter the (**2**) _____, they cause the (**3**) _____ and tiny bones inside the ear to (**4**) _____. Sensors in the inner ear send (**5**) _____ to the brain.

#103. Human Body 19

Circle the best term to fit each clue.

1. Light rays focus on rods and cones here.

   lens   cornea   retina

2. This flexible, clear structure controls focus in the eye.

   lens   cornea   retina

3. This is the colored part of the eye.

   iris   lens   pupil

4. This opening lets light into the eye.

   iris   lens   pupil

5. The clear outside coating of the eye.

   cornea   iris   pupil

#104. Human Body 20

Circle the four basic tastes the taste buds can detect. Write a food for each taste.

1. spicy _____

2. sweet _____

3. sour _____

4. salty _____

5. bitter _____

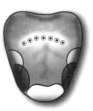

Name: _____ Date: _____

Human Body

#105. Observing the Organization of the Human Body 1

You will need a watch or a clock with a minute hand. Place an index finger either below and just behind your ear or on your wrist until you feel the throb of your pulse. Count the number of pulses per minute three different times. Then average the three numbers.

1. sitting _____
2. standing _____
3. after running in place for 30 seconds

   _____
4. How did your pulse change?

   _____
5. What causes your pulse?

   _____

   _____

#106. Observing the Organization of the Human Body 2

Hold your hands about three inches away from your eyes, and touch your two index fingers together. Now focus on a distant wall while you move your fingers about a half-inch apart. Glance back at your fingers and you will see a "floating finger" between your index fingers!

See if you can explain this optical illusion.

_____

_____

_____

_____

_____

#107. Observing the Organization of the Human Body 3

Using a mirror, open your mouth and look at your teeth. The four front ones on top and bottom are called **incisors**. The pointed teeth just behind them are called "eye teeth," or **canines**. The rest of the teeth are **molars**.

Sketch the shape of these different teeth. Based on their size and shape, what different "jobs" do they have when you eat?

_____

_____

_____

_____

#108. Observing the Organization of the Human Body 4

You will need water, two cotton balls, and rubbing alcohol. Moisten one cotton ball with water and rub on your left forearm. Moisten the other cotton ball with rubbing alcohol and rub on your right forearm.

1. Which forearm feels cooler? _____

2. Why? _____

   _____

3. Why might a doctor have prescribed an

   "alcohol bath" for someone in the past?

   _____

   _____

Name: _____ Date: _____

Human Body

#109. Asking About the Organization of the Human Body 1

What digestive system organ best solves each riddle below? Place the letter of the correct organ on the blank next to each riddle.

1. What has peristaltic waves but no sunny beaches? ____

2. What is small and twisty and a whiz at digestion? ____

3. What is home to friendly microbes and loves to soak up water? ____

> A. pancreas   B. mouth
> C. large intestine   D. small intestine
> E. esophagus

#110. Asking About the Organization of the Human Body 2

What system in the human body…

1. Controls the response to invading microorganisms?

   _____

2. Provides for gas exchange between the air and the body?

   _____

3. Breaks down food and absorbs nutrients?

   _____

4. Provides support and stores minerals?

   _____

#111. Asking About the Organization of the Human Body 3

Write questions that have the following answers.

1. **A, B, O,** and **AB**

   _____

   _____

2. **white blood cells**

   _____

   _____

3. **left** and **right ventricles**

   _____

   _____

#112. Asking About the Organization of the Human Body 4

Find a partner. Each of you write the name of one of the 206 human bones on a piece of paper and put the paper in an envelope. Each of you may ask ten questions that can be answered with a "yes" or a "no."

What are the mystery bones?

Yours:

   _____

Your partner's:

   _____

Name: _____ Date: _____

Human Body

#113. Understanding the Organization of the Human Body 1

Of the 100 trillion cells inside us, only one in ten is human. The rest belong to bacteria, fungi, viruses, and microscopic insects—many of them either "hitchhikers" or **symbionts** performing valuable services to keep us healthy.

1. T or F: All microorganisms  cause disease. _____

2. Organisms that live on or in the human body include _____,

_____,

_____, and

_____.

#114. Understanding the Organization of the Human Body 2

The form of a human cell reflects the function it performs. Muscle cells are long with fibers that contract. Nerve cells have many branches (**dendrites**) and insulated **axons** for transmitting nerve impulses. White blood cells have bumpy extensions that surround foreign invaders.

1. T or F: A skin cell is flat and plate-like to provide protection. _____

2. Muscle cells have fibers that can _____ like an entire muscle.

#115. Understanding the Organization of the Human Body 3

A blocked blood vessel that serves the brain may cause a **stroke**. A blocked blood vessel in the heart starves the heart muscle and causes a **heart attack**. A weak-walled blood vessel may expand into a bulge called an **aneurysm** that may burst.

1. Blood vessels can become blocked in the brain, causing a _____.

2. Blood vessels may burst if an _____ is present.

#116. Understanding the Organization of the Human Body 4

The **central nervous system (CNS)** consists of the brain and spinal cord. The brain is divided into the **medulla** that takes care of "autopilot" functions, the **cerebellum** that handles coordination and balance, and the **cerebrum** that understands passages of text like this one.

1. Use your _____ to read this activity, your _____ to walk to the gym, and your _____ to keep your heart beating.

2. CNS stands for _____

_____ _____.

Name: _____   Date: _____

Human Body

#117. Figuring Out the Organization of the Human Body 1

I live in a bean-shaped organ deep within the body. I filter wastes from the blood while cleverly reabsorbing certain nutrients, salts, and water. I hang around with a bunch of my tubular buddies in a structure called a **capsule**.

What am I? _____

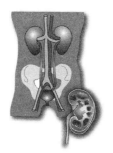

#118. Figuring Out the Organization of the Human Body 2

Match the part of the nervous system with the function it performs.

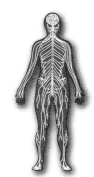

A. **interneurons**
B. **motor neurons**
C. **sensory neurons**
D. **effectors**
E. **spinal cord**

_____ 1. carry out CNS commands.
_____ 2. transmit signals from receptors.
_____ 3. connect sensory and motor neurons.
_____ 4. is the main nerve trunk line.
_____ 5. innervate muscles.

#119. Figuring Out the Organization of the Human Body 3

Microscopic invaders have entered your body. They cruise around in the blood until they find **T-cells**, and then they destroy them.

What will happen in your body if you don't find a way to replace T-cells?

_____

_____

_____

_____

_____

#120. Figuring Out the Organization of the Human Body 4

Next to the following human diseases write I if it is **infectious** and NI if it is not infectious. Be prepared to explain your answers.

1. **diabetes mellitus** _____

2. **scurvy** _____

3. **yellow fever** _____

4. **HIV** _____

5. **cancer** _____

Name: _____ Date: _____

Earth Science

#121. Earth Science 1

Write the best term for each clue.

| outer core | mantle |
| inner core | crust |

1. the outer layer of the earth

   _____

2. the center of the earth

   _____

3. just below the earth's outer layer

   _____

4. layer just above the earth's center

   _____

#122. Earth Science 2

Fill in the missing letters.

1. a crack in the rocky crust

   of the earth: **f __ __ l __**

2. shaking of the earth's surface caused by

   underground movement:

   e __ __ th __ __ a __ e

3. ripple of energy passing through rock,

   water, or air: **w __ v __**

4. machine that records ground movements:

   s __ __ s __ __ g __ __ __ h

#123. Earth Science 3

Draw a line to match each term to the best clue.

1. **seismology**   size

2. **shallow**   shaking

3. **tsunami**   study of
              earthquakes

4. **tremor**   near the surface

5. **magnitude**   ocean wave caused
               by an earthquake

#124. Earth Science 4

Fill in the missing letters.

1. relating to a volcano:

   v __ __ c __ __ ic

2. powdery rock from a volcanic explosion:

   a __ __

3. hard, dark rock formed from cooled lava:

   b __ __ a __ t

4. very light-weight volcanic rock:

   p __ __ i __ e

5. glassy volcanic rock:

   ob __ __ d __ __ n

Name: _____ Date: _____

Earth Science

#125. Earth Science 5

Write the letter for the correct term on each line.

> **A. crater**   **B. chamber**   **C. volcano**
> **D. magma**   **E. vent**

A (**1**) _____ is a cone-shaped mountain.
It forms when (**2**) _____, or molten rock, rises
from a magma (**3**) _____ to the surface. It flows
out through a (**4**) _____ at the top. After the
eruption, the top of the mountain often caves in
to form a (**5**) _____.

#126. Earth Science 6

Circle the term that matches each clue.

1. poisonous:

    toxic   explosive   volcanic

2. able to blow up:

    solidify   explosive   volcanic

3. turn into a solid:

    erupt   shield   solidify

4. outpouring of lava, ash, or gases:

    eruption   shield   composite

#127. Earth Science 7

Draw a line to match each sedimentary rock to
its source.

1. **sandstone**   clay

2. **conglomerate**   sand

3. **shale**   dissolved shells

4. **limestone**   pebbles, sand, and
                           clay

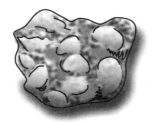

#128. Earth Science 8

Write the best term on each line.

> **resistant   erosion   strata**
> **conservation   weathering**

1. layers of rock: _____

2. removal of rock by water or wind:

    _____

3. breaking up of rock by ice, rain, wind, or

    chemical action: _____

4. protecting soil from overuse or erosion:

    soil _____

5. able to stand up to erosion (a hard rock

    layer): _____

Name: _____ Date: _____

Earth Science

#129. Earth Science 9

The following words are characteristics used to identify rocks and minerals.
Unscramble each term.

1. **lsture** _____

2. **sardhnes** _____

3. **olocr** _____

4. **satkre rlooc** _____

5. **tycrsla pehas** _____

#130. Earth Science 10

Draw a line to match each term with an example.

1. **renewable resource**   wind energy

2. **nonrenewable resource**   smog

3. **alternative energy source**   forests

4. **pollution**   oil

#131. Earth Science 11

Fill in the missing letters.

1. Hard coal that burns at a high temperature

   a __ t __ r __ c __ __ e

2. Soft coal that burns at lower temperatures

   b __ t __ __ i __ o __ s

3. Parts of living things turned to rock, coal, or petroleum

   fo __ __ i __ s

#132. Earth Science 12

Write the letter of the correct word on the line.

| A. topography | B. lithosphere |
| C. block | D. folded |

____ 1. mountains that are pushed up between two faults

____ 2. mountains built from bent rock layers

____ 3. the top rocky layer of the crust

____ 4. the surface features of an area

Name: _____ Date: _____

Earth Science

#133. Earth Science 13

Write the letter of the correct term on the line.

> **A. dunes**   **B. crescent**
> **C. particles**   **D. deposited**

1. Sand _____ come in several shapes.

2. Sand is composed of rock _____.

3. Many dunes are _____- shaped.

4. The sand is carried and _____ by the wind.

#134. Earth Science 14

Unscramble each term.

1. large floating chunk of ice:

   ibeegrc _____

2. melting glacier:

   rtreangeti _____

3. growing glacier:

   acianndvg _____

4. U-shaped area created by a glacier:

   lyeval _____

5. type of glacier that covers large areas of Antarctica:

   cie hsete _____

#135. Earth Science 15

Write the letter for the best term on each line.

> **A. ground water**   **B. columns**
> **C. surface streams**   **D. formations**
> **E. chambers**

Limestone caverns are often filled with beautiful (**1**) _____. Natural (**2**) _____ dissolves the rock to create underground rooms called (**3**) _____. Stalactites, stalagmites, and (**4**) _____ are like magical gardens of stone. Sometimes (**5**) _____ plunge down through openings to form waterfalls.

#136. Earth Science 16

Fill in the missing letters.

1. A consistent flow of surface water is an ocean **c __ __ __ e __ t**.

2. The **d __ __ t __** of the ocean varies from shallow shelves to deep trenches.

3. The saltiness of the ocean is called its **s __ l __ __ __ t __**.

4. The word **m __ r __ __ e** refers to the ocean.

Name: _____   Date: _____

Earth Science

#137. Earth Science 17

Draw a line to match each clue to the correct term.

1. the deepest parts of the ocean floor   **hot spot**

2. not deep   **island**

3. top

4. land surrounded by water   **trenches**

5. place where volcanic islands form   **shallow**

surface

#138. Earth Science 18

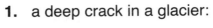

Unscramble each term

1. a deep crack in a glacier:

   sevacres _____

2. to crush:

   mptcaco _____

3. loose rock fragments:

   ebrisd _____

4. large loose rocks:

   oulbders _____

#139. Earth Science 19

Circle T for true or F for false.

T F **1.** **Floodplains** are found on steep mountainsides.

T F **2.** A **delta** forms where a large river enters the ocean.

T F **3.** A river **meander** is an area with many rapids.

T F **4.** A **canyon** is a narrow valley with steep walls.

T F **5.** A **river system** includes the source, the tributaries, and the mouth.

#140. Earth Science 20

Match each term to the best description.

____ **1.** any precious stone   **A. amethyst**

____ **2.** the hardest stone   **B. emerald**

____ **3.** fossilized tree sap   **C. gem**

____ **4.** a purple stone   **D. amber**

____ **5.** a green gem   **E. diamond**

Name: _____ Date: _____

Earth Science

#141. Understanding Earth Materials 1

Minerals fracture or break apart in different ways. Quartz breaks with **conchoidal fractures** like the ridges on seashells. Certain metals show **hackly or jagged fractures**. **Earthy fractures** look powdery in appearance.

1. If a metal breaks with a hackly fracture, you know the edges of the break look _____.

2. Amethyst is a kind of quartz. You can expect it to have _____ fractures.

#142. Understanding Earth Materials 2

The history of life on Earth is divided into three major time periods called **eras**. The **Paleozoic Era** is oldest, and the word means "the age of old life." The **Mesozoic Era**, also called the age of dinosaurs, is the age of "middle life." We live in the **Cenozoic Era**, or age of "new life."

1. Dinosaurs lived during the

   _____ Era.

2. If *zoic* means "life" and *Era* means "age," then *paleo* means _____,

   meso means _____, and

   ceno means _____.

#143. Understanding Earth Materials 3

Scientists have learned that the outermost crust of Earth is broken into a series of very large **tectonic plates** that "float" a few inches every year on the much hotter rocks beneath them. Over the many years of plates colliding with each other, mountain ranges form when the crust folds and wrinkles.

1. Mountain ranges form when

   _____ _____ collide.

2. True or False? Tectonic plates move a few feet every year. _____

#144. Understanding Earth Materials 4

Sometimes rocks fold under pressure. A bulge of rock layers is called an **anticline**, and a dip is called a **syncline**. When rock layers break and slip up or down against each other, the process is called **faulting**, and the slippage area is a **fault**.

1. Hot spots beneath the Earth often cause rock layers to bulge outward and create a(n) _____.

2. A big crack in the Earth where layers of rock no longer line up properly is called a(n) _____.

Name: _____   Date: _____

Earth Science

#145. Figuring Out Earth Materials 1

I am a mineral. I can be black, almost colorless, or anywhere in between. You can pull me apart (ouch!) into sheets as thin as paper. I can be scratched with a penny.

What am I?

_____

#146. Figuring Out Earth Materials 2

I am a mineral. Even if I'm common in the earth's crust, I'm beautiful, if I do say so myself. I possess six-sided crystals and can be colored white, pink, purple, or gray.

What am I?

_____

#147. Figuring Out Earth Materials 3

A mineral? Yes, dear, I certainly am. My crystals are often long and needlelike. I'm usually black, but can be dark green or brown. I look a bit like glass. You can break me into wedge-shaped pieces (although I wouldn't encourage that, you understand). Usually, I can't be scratched with a paper clip.

What am I?

_____

#148. Figuring Out Earth Materials 4

I'm a rock, and don't you forget it. I'm formed hot, and then I cool tough, with a distinguished, salt-and-pepper look. You can polish me up, and I'll look great for many years. In fact, you can make a rather nice monument from me if you want.

What am I?

_____

Name: _____ Date: _____

Earth Science

#149. Finding Out About Earth Materials 1

What happened first? List the following Earth science discoveries in order from the most recent (#1) to the earliest (#5).

_____ **a.** William Smith discovers that certain fossils are always found in certain sedimentary layers.

_____ **b.** Alfred Wegener proposes the idea of **continental drift**.

_____ **c.** The distance and approximate size of the **moon** is first calculated.

_____ **d.** The name "**dinosaur**" is given to certain large, reptile-like creatures.

_____ **e.** The volcano **Krakatoa** erupts, creating the "year without summer."

#150. Finding Out About Earth Materials 2

Research the roles of **Edward Drinker Cope** (1840–1897) and **Othniel Charles Marsh** (1831–1899) in the so-called "**Dinosaur Wars**." You may find the following reference useful: *Fossil Feud* by **Thom Holmes** (1998).

What Colorado teacher helped spark the feud between Cope and Marsh?

_____

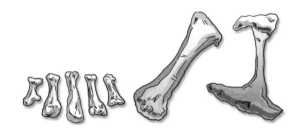

#151. Finding Out About Earth Materials 3

Define the following earth science terms and list your reference sources after each definition.

1. **anthracite** _____

   _____

   _____

2. **bedrock** _____

   _____

   _____

3. **epicenter** _____

   _____

   _____

4. **Pangaea** _____

   _____

   _____

#152. Finding Out About Earth Materials 4

Answer these questions.

1. What do the following terms have in common? **dendrochronology**, **radiocarbon dating**, **relative age,** and **relative dating**

   _____

   _____

   _____

   _____

2. What technique would be most accurate for determining the age of a woolly mammoth tusk? Why?

   _____

   _____

   _____

Name: _____   Date: _____

Earth Science

#153. Observing Ancient Life 1

Fossil teeth can tell scientists a lot about their owner's eating habits. Look at the examples of fossil teeth below. Match the fossil teeth to the animal described. If necessary, find pictures of modern animal teeth like those of cats, elephants, horses, and baleen whales for comparison.

1. a meat eater ___
2. an animal that chewed lots of veggies ___
3. an animal that ate leaves and other coarse vegetation ___
4. an animal that filtered food from the water ___

A.   B.   C.   D.

#154. Observing Ancient Life 2

Animals have developed several different ways to fly.

1. Which animal had a wing made from a single finger? ___
2. Which animal had a wing made from an entire hand? ___
3. Which animal used its entire arm for a wing? ___

A.   B.

C.

#155. Observing Ancient Life 3

Look carefully at the illustration of the allosaurus below and put the letter of the track diagram that fits the animal next to its name.

allosaurus ___

A.

B.

C.

#156. Observing Ancient Life 4

Which fossil organism:

1. looks most like an insect? _____
2. resembles a snail? _____
3. swam in the water? _____
4. ate other animals? _____

A.   B.

C.   D.

Name: _____ Date: _____

Earth Science

#157. Asking About Ancient Life 1

Below are the answers to three questions. Write the question asked for each answer.

1. Answer: **mosasaurs** and **plesiosaurs**

   _____

   _____

2. Answer: **get trapped in amber**, **get petrified**, **get frozen**

   _____

   _____

3. Answer: **Paleozoic**, **Mesozoic**, and **Cenozoic**

   _____

   _____

#158. Asking About Ancient Life 2

Match the question with the correct answer.

> **A. smilodon**   **B. megatherium**
> **C. trilobite**

_____ 1. What ancient ocean animal had a 3-part body, antennae, and calcite eyes?

_____ 2. What ancient mammal was 7 ft. tall at the shoulder and ate tree leaves?

_____ 3. What ancient mammal had sabre teeth?

#159. Asking About Ancient Life 3

At **Cleveland-Lloyd Dinosaur Quarry** in Utah, over 60% of the fossils found are those of the predator, **allosaurus**. Usually prey species far outnumber their predators. Some scientists say this area may have been a **predator trap**—a place where predators were attracted to prey stuck in mud or tar, then got stuck themselves.

List several ways you could test this hypothesis.

_____

_____

_____

_____

_____

#160. Asking About Ancient Life 4

Name the dinosaur to which the riddle refers.

> **A. triceratops**   **B. ankylosaurus**
> **C. ceratosaurus**   **D. maiasaura**

_____ 1. What weighed 4 tons, had a beak, lots of spikes, and could club you with its tail?

_____ 2. What had 3 horns, a neck frill, and a face only a mother could love?

_____ 3. What good mama hadrosaur lived and tended her babies in Montana?

_____ 4. What horny-snouted predator competed with Allosaurus for Apatosaurus steaks?

Name: _____ Date: _____

Earth Science

#161. Understanding Ancient Life 1

Dead plants and animals may be preserved as various kinds of fossils. Elephant relatives called **woolly mammoths** have been frozen and preserved in glacial ice. Many animals have fallen into **tar pits** and bogs.  Insects may get stuck in gooey sap that later turns to **amber**. And when animals are buried quickly and bathed in mineral-carrying water, bone eventually turns to stone.

1. True or False? All fossils are made of stone. _____

2. True or False? Woolly mammoths are related to elephants. _____

#162. Understanding Ancient Life 2

In 1908, **Charles Sternberg** and his sons discovered something amazing: a dinosaur **mummy**. The dinosaur apparently died on a sandbar in an ancient river and dried out, or mummified. Later, it was buried by mud in a flash flood, and its carcass **fossilized**.

1. To become a fossil mummy, a creature must first _____ and then get _____.

2. A dinosaur mummy was discovered by _____.

#163. Understanding Ancient Life 3

Earth has suffered two very big disasters during its years of existence. Over 60% of Earth's species died, including the dinosaurs, when a hunk of space rock hit the Earth. At an earlier time, nearly 90% of Earth's species died for reasons only partially understood.

1. True or False? Dinosaurs died in the first of two big disasters on Earth. _____

2. What percentage of Earth's species died in the first disaster? _____

#164. Understanding Ancient Life 4

Want to become a **fossil** someday? Here's a recipe: 1) Have hard parts like bone or shell. 2) Die in a river, lake, or ocean. 3) Get buried quickly so you don't rot too fast. 4) Have  mineralized water seep around you so you can turn to stone. 5) Get lucky, so you don't get smashed up or eroded away.

1. To become fossilized it helps to die in a _____, _____, or _____.

2. To turn to stone, bones need to have water that contains _____.

Name: _____ Date: _____

Earth Science

#165. Figuring Out Ancient Life 1

What lived during the last ice age, had extra long legs, was bigger than a sabre-toothed cat, but just as hairy, and has a modern relative named "Smokey"?

_____

#166. Figuring Out Ancient Life 2

What lived in Montana many years ago, was as big as a double-decker bus, had foot-long teeth, and is nicknamed "Sue"?

_____

#167. Figuring Out Ancient Life 3

What traveled in packs, was about 3 feet long, sometimes ate a friend when the going got tough, and was the great-great-granddaddy (or grandmommy) of many of the later, meat-eating dinosaurs? (*Hint:* Some of them were "rounded up" at a ghost ranch in New Mexico.)

_____

#168. Figuring Out Ancient Life 4

What flew like a bird (but wasn't), is often confused with dinosaurs (but isn't), and probably was hairy (but isn't named Harry)?

_____

Name: _____ Date: _____

Atmospheric Science

#169. Atmospheric Science 1

Circle T for true or F for false.

T F **1.** **Air pressure** is the weight of air pushing down.

T F **2.** Falling rain is an example of **evaporation**.

T F **3.** The earth's **atmosphere** is composed of gases.

T F **4.** The **weather** is the current condition of outdoor air.

T F **5.** A rainstorm is an example of **climate**.

#170. Atmospheric Science 2

Draw a line to match each instrument to what it measures.

1. **anemometer**   air pressure

2. **barometer**   temperature

3. **hygrometer**   precipitation

4. **thermometer**   humidity

5. **rain gauge**   wind speed

#171. Atmospheric Science 3

Circle the term that matches each clue.

1. long dry period:

   pollution   ozone   drought

2. greenhouse effect:

   global warming

   global cooling

   pollution

3. a form of oxygen:

   nitrogen   drought   ozone

4. man-made impurities:

   pollution   nitrogen   ozone

5. world-wide:

   local   coastal   global

#172. Atmospheric Science 4

Write the correct term from the box on each line.

> warm front   transpiration   cold front
> El Niño   evaporation

1. a warm ocean current that creates unusual weather _____

2. a cool air mass moving in on a warm air mass _____

3. a warm air mass moving in on a cool air mass _____

4. water vapor moving into the air through the leaves of plants

   _____

5. to change from a liquid to a gas

   _____

Name: _____ Date: _____

Atmospheric Science

#173. Atmospheric Science 5

Circle T for true or F for false.

T F **1.** A **droplet** is a very large water drop.

T F **2.** **Fog** consists of water droplets suspended in the air.

T F **3.** **Smog** is fog mixed with smoke or other pollutants.

T F **4.** A **drizzle** is a heavy downpour.

T F **5.** If the air is **moist**, it is extremely dry.

#174. Atmospheric Science 6

Unscramble the terms.

1. light waves invisible to humans, used in remote controls:

nfridare _____

2. different forms of the same thing:

rinsativao _____

3. an element present in living things:

arbnco _____

4. to move around:

ctelircua _____

#175. Atmospheric Science 7

Circle the correct term to match the definition.

1. high clouds, often made of ice:

cumulus   stratus   cirrus

2. low, fluffy-looking clouds:

cumulus   stratus   cirrus

3. an even blanket of low gray clouds:

cumulus   stratus   cirrus

4. mid-level clouds in bunches:

altocumulus cirrus   nimbus

5. rainclouds:

altocumulus cirrus   nimbus

#176. Atmospheric Science 8

Unscramble each term.

1. rain, hail, and snow:

pipitaorectin _____

2. repeating periods of heat and cold:

weather **tprnate** _____

3. ice chunks: **ihla** _____

4. ice crystals: **nsow** _____

5. liquid water drops: **arin** _____

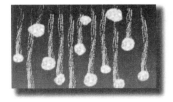

Name: _____ Date: _____

Atmospheric Science

#177. The Atmosphere 1

Write a good definition of **atmosphere**.

_____

_____

_____

_____

_____

_____

#178. The Atmosphere 2

Write T for true or F for false.

1. ____ The atmosphere is like a blanket of air surrounding the earth.

2. ____ The atmosphere is over two miles high.

3. ____ The atmosphere retains heat at night.

4. ____ The atmosphere protects us from the sun's UV rays.

5. ____ The air in the atmosphere gets thicker as you go higher.

#179. The Atmosphere 3

Unscramble the names of these things that make up the atmosphere.

1. G N R T O I N E _____

2. Y N X O E G _____

3. T R A W E   P O V R A

   _____

4. R A O N B C   I X D I D O E

   _____

5. R H T O E   S G A E S

   _____

6. S U D T _____

#180. The Atmosphere 4

Number these layers of the atmosphere from the closest to the earth (1) to the farthest up (4).

1. _____ **mesosphere**

2. _____ **troposphere**

3. _____ **thermosphere**

4. _____ **stratosphere**

Circle the layer of the atmosphere that is split into the **ionosphere** and the **exosphere**.

Name: _____   Date: _____

Atmospheric Science

#181. The Atmosphere 5

Fill in the blanks with words from the box.

rotation	unevenly	move
wind	weather	heats

_____ happens

because the sun _____ the

earth _____. This causes

the air and clouds to _____

all the time. The sun's heat, combined with the

earth's _____, creates

global _____ patterns.

#182. The Atmosphere 6

Change the underlined words to make the information correct.

The troposphere is the layer of the

atmosphere <u>farthest from</u> the earth. It goes up

about six <u>meters</u>. Here is where almost all of

Earth's <u>meteors</u> occur. The temperature in the

troposphere <u>increases</u> as you go higher up. At

the top of the troposphere is an area where the

temperature doesn't drop any more. It is called

the <u>tropostop</u>.

#183. The Atmosphere 7

1. Which layer of the atmosphere has most of Earth's weather?

   _____

2. Which atmospheric layer reflects radio waves back to Earth?

   _____

3. In which layer of the atmosphere do most planes fly?

   _____

4. In which atmospheric layer do most meteoroids break up?

   _____

#184. The Atmosphere 8

What layer of the atmosphere am I?

_____

Clue one: I begin about 6 to 10 miles above the Earth.

Clue two: My upper layer traps **ozone**, which protects from the sun's **UV rays**.

Clue three: Planes like to fly here because there are few clouds or weather to bump them around.

Name: _____ Date: _____

Atmospheric Science

#185. Air Pressure 1

Fill in the blanks with words from the box.

| amount | temperature | earth |
| gravity | pressure | weight |

_____ acts on air and

pulls it toward the _____.

The _____ of the air

being pulled down on an area of the earth

is called air _____. Air

pressure is affected by two things: the

_____ of air above it and

_____.

#186. Air Pressure 2

Write *Yes* or *No* to indicate if each statement is correct.

1. _____ Warm air weighs more than cold air.

2. _____ **Air pressure** sometimes changes very quickly.

3. _____ The particles in cold air are tighter together than in warm air.

4. _____ Air will move as quickly as it can from an area of **high pressure** to  an area of **low pressure**.

#187. Air Pressure 3

Circle which in each pair would have greater air pressure.

1. A beach at sea level

   The top of a mountain

2. The equator

   The South Pole

3. A cold, snowy day

   A hot, sunny day

4. The stratosphere

   The thermosphere

#188. Air Pressure 4

Circle the correct term in each set of parentheses to complete each sentence.

1. Although **high pressure** is caused by (warm / cold) air, it results in (good / bad) weather.

2. Although **low pressure** is caused by (warm / cold) air, it results in (good / bad) weather.

Name: _____ Date: _____

Atmospheric Science

#189. Heat 1

Match the term to the correct definition.

> **A. radiation**
> **B. conduction**
> **C. convection**

1. _____ transfer of heat by movement of a fluid

2. _____ transfer of heat from one substance to another

3. _____ direct transfer of energy by electromagnetic waves

#190. Heat 2

Write T for true or F for false.

1. ____ Cooler, denser air sinks toward the ground, pushing warmer air up.

2. ____ **Convection currents** move heat in the **troposphere**.

3. ____ All heat radiated by the sun enters the **atmosphere**.

4. ____ The atmosphere stops heat from escaping to space.

#191. Heat 3

Explain how the angle at which sunlight strikes the earth affects the average temperatures at areas near the equator and the poles.

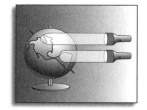

_____

_____

_____

_____

_____

_____

#192. Heat 4

Fill in the blanks with words from the box.

> rise   sinks   movement
> slow   dense   molecules

In hot air, _____ move faster and farther apart, making the air less _____. In cool air, molecules _____, making it more dense.

Denser air _____, making the less-dense air _____. This creates _____ of the air.

Name: _____ Date: _____

Atmospheric Science

#193. Winds 1

Fill in the blanks.

1. All surface wind is caused by differences in A_____ P_____.

2. Wind is the horizontal movement of air from an area of H_____ pressure to an area of L_____ pressure.

3. Most differences in air pressure are caused by unequal H_____ in the atmosphere.

#194. Winds 2

What am I? _____

Clue one: I am an instrument to measure wind speed.

Clue two: I have three or four cups mounted at the ends of spokes, which spin as the wind blows.

Clue three: A speedometer attached to my axle will show the wind speed.

#195. Winds 3

Circle the correct word from each set.

1. The name of a wind tells where the wind is (going to / coming from).

2. A south wind blows (from / to) the south (from / to) the north.

3. Air moves from areas of (higher / lower) pressure to areas of (higher / lower) pressure.

#196. Winds 4

Which winds are described in each statement?

1. Calm area where warm air rises

   _____

2. These winds blow toward the equator.

   _____

3. These winds blow away from the poles.

   _____

4. These winds blow away from the 30 degree latitudes (or horse latitudes).

   _____

Name: _____   Date: _____

Atmospheric Science

#197. Water in the Atmosphere 1

List an example of water in each state listed below:

1. gaseous _____

2. liquid _____

3. solid _____

#198. Water in the Atmosphere 2

Match.

A. humidity	B. evaporation
C. relative humidity	D. psychrometer

1. _____ the process by which water enters the atmosphere

2. _____ the instrument used to measure relative humidity

3. _____ the amount of water vapor in the air

4. _____ the percentage of water vapor in the air compared to the maximum the air could hold

#199. Water in the Atmosphere 3

Unscramble these places from which water evaporates.

1. S O E C A N _____

2. S L D U D E P _____

3. V S L A E E _____

4. T S M E R A S _____

5. D S N P O _____

6. E S A S _____

7. I L S O _____

8. K S L E A _____

#200. Water in the Atmosphere 4

Fill in the blanks with words from the box.

water vapor	crystals	atmosphere
liquid	less	condensation

Cold air can hold _____ water vapor than warm air. Clouds form when _____ in the air becomes _____ water or ice _____. This process is called _____. When warm air rises into the _____, some of the water vapor forms clouds.

Name: _____ Date: _____

Atmospheric Science

#201. Water in the Atmosphere 5

Match.

> A. frost
> B. dew
> C. dew point
> D. ice crystals

1. _____ the temperature at which conden-

    sation begins

2. _____ water condensed on a cold surface

3. _____ ice deposited onto a cold surface

4. _____ frozen water vapor

#202. Water in the Atmosphere 6

Use these terms to label the diagram of the water cycle. Briefly explain the process of each part to the class.

evaporation   condensation   precipitation

#203. Water in the Atmosphere 7

Match.

1. _____ fluffy, heap-like   **A. cirrus**
    clouds

2. _____ low and gray   **B. stratus**
    clouds that bring
    precipitation   **C. cumulus**

3. _____ high-level, wispy,
    feathery clouds   **D. nimbus**

4. _____ flat, layered
    clouds that cover
    most of the sky

#204. Water in the Atmosphere 8

1. Which types of clouds

    bring thunderstorms?

    _____

2. Which types of clouds are made up mostly of

    ice crystals? _____

3. Which types of clouds often bring periods

    of drizzling rain or snow?

    _____

4. Any cloud that produces precipitation is

    called this: _____

Name: _____ Date: _____

Atmospheric Science

#205. Precipitation 1

Define **precipitation**: _____

_____

_____

Give examples of three types of precipitation.

1. _____
2. _____
3. _____

#206. Precipitation 2

Write T for true or F for false.

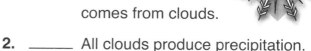

1. _____ Precipitation always comes from clouds.

2. _____ All clouds produce precipitation.

3. _____ Precipitation occurs when clouds get high enough.

4. _____ Snow is a form of precipitation.

5. _____ Raindrops are smaller than cloud droplets.

#207. Precipitation 3

Match.

| A. rain | B. sleet | C. snow |
| D. hail | E. freezing rain | |

1. _____ drops freeze when they touch a cold surface and ice builds up
2. _____ round pellets formed during a thunderstorm
3. _____ drops of water at least 0.5 millimeters in diameter
4. _____ drops frozen into solid ice particles (less than 5 mm) as they fall
5. _____ water vapor converted directly into six-sided ice crystals

#208. Precipitation 4

1. What is the most common form of precipitation?

_____

2. Snowflakes are clear. What makes them look white? _____

_____

_____

3. What device is used to measure the amount of rainfall that occurs in a particular area at a certain time? _____

Name: _____ Date: _____

Atmospheric Science

#209. Air Masses & Fronts 1

Fill in the blanks.

An air mass is a huge body of air that has similar air P_____, similar T_____, and similar H_____. It can cover an area as large as one M_____ square kilometers.

#210. Air Masses & Fronts 2

Unscramble these four weather factors.

1. RAI SPURESER

_____

2. PMTEUERTRAE

_____

3. NDIW RNCTOIDEI

_____

4. SETMUOIR

_____

#211. Air Masses & Fronts 3

Draw a line to match the air masses to their descriptions.

1. **tropical**   forms over land; dry

2. **polar**   forms over oceans; humid

3. **maritime**   forms over the tropics; warm

4. **continental**   forms north or south of 50-degree latitudes; cold

#212. Air Masses & Fronts 4

Write T for true or F for false.

1. _____ **Air masses** are moved by the global wind currents.

2. _____ **Fronts** are places where two different air masses collide.

3. _____ Colliding air masses cause storms.

4. _____ Different types of air masses mix easily.

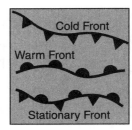

Name: _____ Date: _____

Atmospheric Science

#213. Air Masses & Fronts 5

Write *Yes* or *No* to indicate if each item about a **cold front** is correct.

Cold Front

1. _____ A cold front moves quickly and can bring abrupt weather changes.

2. _____ A cold front occurs when a cold air mass runs into a warm air mass and the cold, dense air slides under the warm air, forcing it up and cooling it off.

3. _____ A cold front always brings rain or snow.

4. _____ Cool, dry air and clear skies often occur after a cold front moves through.

#214. Air Masses & Fronts 6

Circle the word that makes each sentence true.

1. Warm air fronts move more (quickly / slowly) than cold air fronts.

2. The first indicator of an oncoming **warm front** may be (cirrus / stratus) clouds in the sky.

3. In winter, warm fronts bring (snow / sunshine).

Warm Front

#215. Air Masses & Fronts 7

1. What type of front forms when two air masses meet and neither one has enough force to move the other?

_____

2. What kind of weather often results if this front remains stalled over an area?

_____

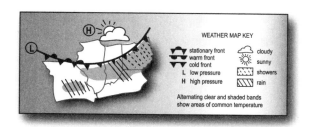

#216. Air Masses & Fronts 8

Write C for **cyclone** or AC for **anticyclone**.

1. _____ a high-pressure center of dry air that spins clockwise (in the northern hemisphere), often bringing dry, clear weather

2. _____ a swirling center of low pressure, spinning counter-clockwise (in the northern hemisphere), often bringing precipitation

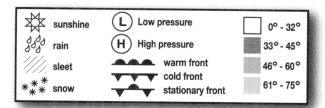

Name: _____   Date: _____

Atmospheric Science

#217. Storms 1

Circle the word in parentheses that makes each sentence true.

1. **Thunderstorms** form within (altostratus / cumulonimbus) clouds.

2. Thunderstorms form when warm air (falls / rises) rapidly and cools.

3. Thunderstorms bring (heavy / light) rain and hail.

#218. Storms 2

What am I? _____

Clue one: I am a sudden discharge of positive and negative electrical charges that build up in a storm.

Clue two: I heat the air to 54,000 degrees Fahrenheit.

Clue three: I kill around 100 people every year in the United States.

#219. Storms 3

Fill in the missing letters.

1. Another name for a tornado is a

    t __ __ s __ __ __.

2. A tornado that forms over the sea or a lake is called a **w __ __ __ r s __ __ __ t**.

3. A swirling storm of sand in the desert is called a **d __ __ __   d __ __ __ __**.

#220. Storms 4

Circle the correct answer.

desending air
funnel cloud-spiral updraft

1. Which is a more likely speed of the wind in a **tornado**?

    45 mph   370 mph

2. How long do most tornadoes stay on the ground?

    A few minutes   A few hours

3. Why do **waterspouts** spin more slowly than tornadoes?

    Water is heavier than air.

    Warmer air spins slower.

Name: _____ Date: _____

Atmospheric Science

#221. Storms 5

Write T for true or F for false.

1. _____ **Tornadoes** are more common in the United States than anywhere else.

2. _____ Tornadoes are the most violent concentration of energy that the atmosphere can produce.

3. _____ Tornadoes occur mostly in the fall and winter.

4. _____ Tornadoes can lift trains off the tracks.

#222. Storms 6

Match the tropical storm with its location.

A. hurricane   B. typhoon
C. cyclone

1. _____ over the Pacific Ocean

2. _____ over the Indian Ocean

3. _____ over the Atlantic Ocean

#223. Storms 7

Fill in the blanks with words from the box.

| winds | land | hurricane |
| tropical | low | spinning |

A _____ begins over

warm, _____ water when

strong _____ blow into an area

of _____ pressure and start

_____ rapidly. They pick up

speed until they reach

_____.

#224. Storms 8

Circle the word in the parentheses that makes each sentence about a storm's center correct.

1. The (lower / higher) the air pressure at the center of a storm, the (slower / faster) the winds blow toward the center.

2. The (highest / lowest) air pressure and the (coolest / warmest) temperatures are at the (center / edge) of the storm.

Name: _____ Date: _____

Space Science

#225. Space Science 1

Unscramble each term.

1. a small rocky body orbiting the sun:

   teroidas _____

2. an icy body with a long tail orbiting the sun:

   otcme _____

3. rock or metal from space entering the earth's atmosphere:

   eormet _____

4. part of a meteor that lands on earth:

   etemoriet _____

#226. Space Science 2

Fill in the missing letters.

1. a group of bright stars associated with a story: **c __ __ st __ __ la __ i __ n**

2. a large group of stars: **g __ l __ __ y**

3. a large sphere of burning gas in space:

   s __ __ __

4. a collapsed star with extremely powerful gravity: **b __ __ __ k h __ __ e**

#227. Space Science 3

Circle the term that best fits each clue.

1. Mars, Venus, Earth:

   outer planets   inner planets

2. revolve around another body:

   orbit   collapse

3. Neptune, Saturn, Jupiter:

   outer planets   inner planets

4. a large body circling a star:

   comet   planet

#228. Space Science 4

Fill in the missing letters.

The four **(1) __ n __ er**

p __ __ n __ __ s are also called the

(2) r __ __ __ y, or terrestrial, planets. They

are **(3) M __ __ c __ r __**,

(4) V __ __ __ __, **(5) E __ __ __ __**,

and **(6) M __ __ __**.

Name: _____ Date: _____

Space Science

#229. Space Science 5

Fill in the missing letters.

The four (**1**) __ **u** __ **e** __ planets are also called the (**2**) **g** __ **s** __ **o** __ **s** planets. They are (**3**) **J** __ **p** __ **t** __ **r**, (**4**) **S** __ **t** __ **r** __, (**5**) **U** __ __ **n** __ **s**, and (**6**) **N** __ __ **t** __ __ **e**.

#230. Space Science 6

Draw a line to match each clue to the best term.

1. our galaxy   **telescope**

2. instrument to see distant objects   **local group**

       nebula

3. grouped close together

4. galaxies close to the Milky Way   **Milky Way**

       cluster

5. a cloud of stars, gas, and dust in space

#231. Space Science 7

Write the letter of the best word on each line.

> **A. Hemisphere**   **B. equator**
> **C. seasons**   **D. tilt**

The (**1**) _____ of the earth's axis causes the (**2**) _____. When it is winter in the Northern (**3**) _____, it is summer in the Southern Hemisphere. The (**4**) _____ separates the Northern Hemisphere from the Southern Hemisphere.

#232. Space Science 8

Circle the term that best fits each clue.

1. a rotating neutron star:

    supernova   pulsar

2. a stage in the death of a medium-sized star:

    red giant   neutron star

3. the sudden brief explosion of a star:

    pulsar   supernova

4. a bright object at the edge of the universe:

    red giant   quasar

Name: _____ Date: _____

Space Science

#233. Space Science 9

Unscramble each boldface term.

1. Cooler dark spots on the surface of the sun are called **otnssups**.

   _____

2. A powerful explosion in the sun's atmosphere is a solar **elfar**.

   _____

3. During a total solar eclipse, the sun's **roacno** _____ is visible.

4. When the moon comes between the sun and the earth, there is a solar **lipeesc**. _____

5. The invisible light waves responsible for sunburns are called **oleurtavilt** _____ rays.

#234. Space Science 10

Place the letter of the term next to the correct definition.

> A. astronomer   B. imaginary
> C. Orion   D. constellation
> E. Ursa Major

____ 1. group of stars connected with a story

____ 2. scientist who studies stars

____ 3. mythic

____ 4. constellation, the great bear

____ 5. constellation, the hunter

#235. Space Science 11

Fill in the missing letters.

1. very small planets, including Pluto:

   d __ a __ f planets

2. an area at the edge of the solar system:

   K __ __ p __ r b __ __ t

3. An area of space between Mars and Jupiter: a __ __ e __ __ id b __ __ t

4. a crater caused by a meteorite:

   __ __ __ a __ t crater

5. Objects in space: b __ __ __ __ s

#236. Space Science 12

Place the letter of the correct word in each blank.

> A. lunar   B. eclipse   C. moon
> D. phases   E. quarter

The **(1)** ____ rotates around the earth. The word **(2)** ____ is an adjective that means "relating to the moon." The moon's shapes, or **(3)** ____, include full, half, and **(4)** ____. Sometimes, the shadow of the earth causes a strange phenomenon called an **(5)** ____.

Name: _____ Date: _____

Space Science

#237. Asking About Astronomy & Space Science 1

Planetary riddles: Name the planet to which the riddle refers.

1. What is banded, full of gas, and marked with a Great Red Spot? _____

2. What has more rings than a bathtub and could float like a rubber ducky?

    _____

3. What has two moons, "canali", and a warrior's name? _____

4. What named for a goddess, very bright, and shows many phases? _____

#238. Asking About Astronomy & Space Science 2

Match the question with the correct term.

> A. meteorites   B. comets
> C. meteors   D. novas

_____ 1. What rare objects in the night sky appear to have wispy tails?

_____ 2. What objects in the night sky appear as brief streaks and may occur in "showers"?

_____ 3. What objects strike the earth after their trip through the atmosphere?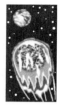

_____ 4. What objects appear suddenly as "new stars," but eventually fade from view?

#239. Asking About Astronomy & Space Science 3

Make up a riddle to describe the following planets. Try them out on a friend.

1. **Mercury** _____
   _____
   _____

2. **Uranus** _____
   _____
   _____

3. **Neptune** _____
   _____
   _____

4. **Earth** _____
   _____
   _____

#240. Asking About Astronomy & Space Science 4

Draw a line from the question on the left to the proper spacecraft on the right.

1. What was the first spacecraft to orbit Earth?

    A. _Apollo 11_

2. What spacecraft arrived at Saturn in 2004?

    B. _Vostok 1_

3. What spacecraft took Neil Armstrong to the moon?

    C. _Viking 1_

4. What spacecraft sent the first pictures from Mars?

    D. _Cassini_

Name: _____ Date: _____

Space Science

#241. Understanding Astronomy & Space Science 1

Our planet, **Earth**, is one of eight planets orbiting a pretty average, yellow star we call the **sun**. The sun contains most of the mass of the solar system. It would take 333,000 Earths to equal the sun's mass.

1. Not counting Earth, there are _____

   other planets in our solar system.

2. As stars go, our sun is _____

   and burns with a _____ light.

#242. Understanding Astronomy & Space Science 2

Venus is a planet closer to the sun than Earth, but nearly the same size. For this reason, Venus is sometimes called Earth's sister planet, even though its atmosphere contains poisonous clouds of sulfuric acid and lead that would melt on its surface.

1. True or False? Venus is called Earth's

   sister planet because it is pretty similar in

   every way. _____

2. True or False? Venus is closer to the sun

   and about the same size as Earth. _____

#243. Understanding Astronomy & Space Science 3

The *Cassini* spacecraft took seven years to travel 3.5 billion miles from Earth to the ringed planet **Saturn**. Early pictures show that Saturn's rings have many dark and light bands not visible from Earth.

1. Earth telescopes cannot see all the details

   in Saturn's _____.

2. If *Cassini* arrived at

   Saturn in 2004, it was

   launched in the year

   _____.

#244. Understanding Astronomy & Space Science 4

In 1612, **Galileo**, one of the first scientists to use a telescope, saw spots on the surface of the sun that changed positions from day to day, disappeared, and then reappeared later. He concluded that the sun rotates on its axis like Earth.

1. A clue to the sun's behavior came from

   observing _____.

2. Telescopes were

   a new scientific

   tool used by

   _____.

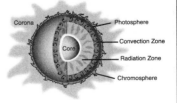

Name: _____   Date: _____

Space Science

#245. Figuring Out Astronomy & Space Science 1

Scientists say reaching planets in a nearby solar system might be technically possible in a few years, but it could take 200 years to get there (traveling at 30,000 km/sec). A crew might consist of 40 to 50 couples whose great-great-grandchildren would finish the trip.

On your own paper, explain why scientists made the following predictions:

- After 200 years, many words in the crew's language (like "horse" and "truck," for example) would have no meaning.

- The people chosen for the original crew should be "motivated, tolerant, and nice people."

#246. Figuring Out Astronomy & Space Science 2

Scientists have discovered what appear to be dried-up river channels on the planet **Mars**. Many places on Mars also show **craters** formed many millions of years ago by collisions with **meteors**. Few of these craters are found near the dry river beds.

Explain how this fact helps support the idea that Mars had liquid water in the not-too-distant past.

_____

_____

_____

_____

_____

#247. Figuring Out Astronomy & Space Science 3

The planet **Venus** seems to move steadily across the night sky during the course of a year. **Mars**, however, moves steadily for a while, slows down, backs up, then moves forward again. (This is called **retrograde motion**.)

Explain why this happens. (*Hint:* Think about the relative positions of Venus, Earth, and Mars in the solar system.)

_____

_____

_____

_____

_____

#248. Figuring Out Astronomy & Space Science 4

All the objects that orbit our local star, the **sun**—things like **asteroids**, **planets**, and **comets**—though they are far away, are much closer than the other stars we see in the sky.

Explain how scientists can often find new asteroids in our solar system by comparing photographs of the same part of the night sky taken several days apart.

_____

_____

_____

_____

_____

Name: _____ Date: _____

Physical Science

#249. Physical Science 1

Fill in the missing letters.

1. colors in white light: **sp __ __ t __ __ m**

2. wavelengths between light and radio waves: **i __ __ __ ar __ d**

3. invisible waves that cause sunburns: **ul __ __ a __ __ ol __ t**

4. colorful arc in sky created by refraction: **r __ __ n __ __ w**

5. the study of light: **o __ __ i __ s**

#250. Physical Science 2

Circle the best term for each clue.

1. practical knowledge:

    fiber   technology   consumption

2. thread:

    metal   gas   fiber

3. iron:

    nonmetal   metal   fiber

4. carbon:

    nonmetal   metal   gas

5. precious metal:

    iron   tin   gold

#251. Physical Science 3

Circle the best term for each clue.

1. a lens curved inward:

    concave   convex   hollow

2. a lens curved outward:

    concave   convex   hollow

3. ability to soak up:

    refraction   reflection   absorption

4. wave changes direction:

    refraction   reflection   absorption

5. wave bounces from a surface:

    refraction   reflection   absorption

#252. Physical Science 4

Draw a line to match each clue to the correct term.

1. enlarge   **telescope**

2. instrument to see   **lens**
    faraway things
                                     binoculars
3. instrument to see
    very small things   **microscope**

                                     magnify
4. instrument with two
    enlarging lenses

5. glass curved to
    bend light

Name: _____ Date: _____

Physical Science

#253. Physical Science 5

Circle T for true or F for false.

T F **1.** The **speed of sound** is faster than the **speed of light**.

T F **2.** **Vibration** is fast side-to-side movement.

T F **3.** The loudness or softness of a musical note is its **pitch**.

T F **4.** A **sonic boom** happens when an airplane goes faster than the speed of sound.

T F **5.** When you travel at a **subsonic speed**, you are underwater.

T F **6.** When you travel at a **supersonic speed**, you are in a slow car.

#254. Physical Science 6

Fill in the missing letters.

1. to swing back and forth rhythmically:

   o __ ci __ __ a __ __

2. extreme point on a pendulum swing:

   a __ __ li __ u __ e

3. repeating: r __ __ e __ __ t __ on

4. number of times something happens in a given amount of time:

   f __ __ __ u __ __ c __

#255. Physical Science 7

Circle the best term for each example.

1. iron:

   metal   alloy   nonmetal

2. molten:

   metal   melted   feathery

3. quartz:

   metal   alloy   nonmetal

4. studies metals:

   geologist   metallurgist

5. brass:

   nonmetal   alloy   copper

#256. Physical Science 8

Circle the numbers of the statements that are true.

1. H_2O is the **chemical formula** for water.

2. Flammability is an example of a **chemical property**.

3. An ice cube melting is a **chemical change**.

4. Water evaporating is a **physical change**.

5. Length is an example of a **physical property**.

Name: _____ Date: _____

Physical Science

#257. Physical Science 9

Fill in the missing letters.

1. A c __ __ p __ n __ __ t is part of something.

2. A c __ mp __ __ n __ is a chemical combination of elements.

3. In a m __ __ t __ __ e, substances combine without a chemical reaction.

4. Salt dissolved in water is a
s __ l __ t __ __ n.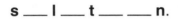

5. Muddy water is a
su __ p __ ns __ __ n.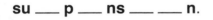

#258. Physical Science 10

Circle the best term for each description.

1. oxygen in the air:

   liquid　　　solid　　　gas

2. water at room temperature:

   liquid　　　solid　　　gas

3. ice:

   liquid　　　solid　　　gas

4. to change from solid to liquid:

   solidify　　evaporate　　melt

5. to change from liquid to solid:

   solidify　　evaporate　　melt

#259. Physical Science 11

Fill in each blank with a term from the box.

> element　　atom　　properties
> molecule　　periodic table

1. An _____ has a nucleus and electrons.

2. A water _____ has two hydrogen atoms and one oxygen atom.

3. Hydrogen is an _____. All of its atoms are hydrogen atoms.

4. The _____ is a chart showing all of the elements.

5. Water has important physical and chemical _____.

#260. Physical Science 12

Use the clues to unscramble each term.

1. draw toward: **tatactr** _____

2. push away: **perel** _____

3. indicates magnetic north:

   mpacsos _____

4. plus: **opvesiti** _____

5. minus: **egiveatn** _____

Name: _____   Date: _____

Physical Science

#261. Physical Science 13

Match the letter of each term to its definition.

_____ 1. a positively charged particle

_____ 2. a particle, neither positively nor negatively charged

_____ 3. the center of an atom

_____ 4. unit of matter (atom, molecule, proton)

_____ 5. substance

A. neutron
B. proton
C. particle
D. nucleus
E. matter

#262. Physical Science 14

Write the letter for the best word on each line.

A. current   B. conductor   C. amp
D. battery

1. An _____ is a basic unit of electricity.

2. A _____ changes chemical energy into electrical energy.

3. Copper is a good _____ of electricity.

4. Electrical _____ flows through the wires.

#263. Physical Science 15

Unscramble each term.

1. route of electrical flow:

   ircuict _____

2. safety device to cut the flow of electricity:

   circuit **abrreke** _____

3. device that reduces or prevents flow of electricity:

   utlainsor _____

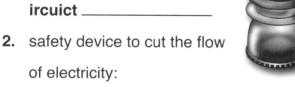

#264. Physical Science 16

Fill in the missing letters.

1. speed up: **a __ __ el __ r __ te**

2. slow down: **d __ c __ l __ r __ t __**

3. speed in a certain direction:

   v __ l __ c __ t __

4. forward motion and resistance to slowing:

   m __ __ e __ t __ m

Name: _____ Date: _____

Physical Science

#265. Physical Science 17

Unscramble each term

1. energy of a moving object:

   etinikc _____

2. unmoving: **ranaoytist** _____

3. changing energy from one form to another:

   onvcoersin _____

4. energy of an object at rest:

   tienptaol _____

#266. Physical Science 18

Fill in the missing letters.

1. Extra heat given off by machines as they

   work is **w __ __ __ e** heat.

2. Energy cannot be created or

   d __ __ tr __ y __ d.

3. **H __ __ t** is a form of energy.

4. **H __ dr __ __ l __ __ tr __ __ __ ty**

   is water power.

#267. Physical Science 19

Circle the best definition
for each term.

1. **work**:

   sweat   transfer energy

2. **generate**:

   create   use

3. **renewable**:

   irreplaceable   replaceable

4. **additional**:

   supplemental   mathematical

#268. Physical Science 20

Match the letter of the term to the correct
definition.

____ 1. ability to do work   **A. friction**

____ 2. stops or moves an   **B. inertia**
           object
                                              C. energy
____ 3. resistance between   **D. force**
           two moving objects
                                              E. motion
____ 4. movement

____ 5. resisting change

Name: _____ Date: _____

Physical Science

#269. Observing Matter & Energy 1

Every object has certain **specific properties**—characteristics that we can describe with our five senses: sight, hearing, smell, touch, and taste.

List five specific properties of your left hand—one property using each sense:

1. _____

2. _____

3. _____

4. _____

5. _____

#270. Observing Matter & Energy 2

Matter exists in different **phases**, either as a **solid**, **liquid**, or **gas**.

In which phase will you most likely find the following substances in your classroom?

1. sweat _____

2. chocolate bar _____

3. milk _____

4. nitrogen _____

5. hand lotion _____

6. hair _____

7. carbon dioxide _____

8. water _____

#271. Observing Matter & Energy 3

Moving or changing matter requires **energy**. Common kinds of energy are chemical, heat, sound, electricity, and light.

Name five sources of energy in your classroom:

1. _____

2. _____

3. _____

4. _____

5. _____

#272. Observing Matter & Energy 4

Mass is the amount of matter in an object. Number the following objects from 1 to 5, with 1 being the object with the least mass and 5 the object having the most mass.

A. ____   B. ____

C. ____    D. ____

E. ____

Name: _____ Date: _____

Physical Science

#273. Understanding Matter & Energy 1

Mass refers to the amount of matter an object has. A whale has more mass than a skunk. Mass resists being moved. This resistance is called **inertia**. Try pushing both a whale and a skunk, and you will find that the whale has more inertia. Mass is measured in units of grams or kilograms in the metric system.

1. An object's resistance to motion is called _____.

2. You could measure the mass of your shoe in _____.

3. Mass is the amount of _____ an object has.

#274. Understanding Matter & Energy 2

Elements are the simplest form of pure substances. They cannot be changed into anything simpler by chemical means. **Compounds** are pure substances composed of two or more elements. **Chemical reactions** occur when compounds are formed or broken down.

1. Chemical reactions cannot change or break down _____.

2. When the elements sodium and chlorine combine, they form a _____ called **table salt**.

#275. Understanding Matter & Energy 3

Dmitri Mendeleev organized all the elements known in 1869 by listing them in a table of increasing **atomic masses**. He found that the elements tended to fall into groups whose **physical** and **chemical properties** varied in a regular or periodic way.

⁵ B Boron 10.811	⁶ C Carbon 12.011	⁷ N Nitrogen 14.007
¹³ Al Aluminum 26.982	¹⁴ Si Silicon 28.806	¹⁵ P Phosphorus 30.974

1. When arranged by atomic masses, elements fall into groups with other elements with _____ physical and chemical properties.

2. What is this table called?

_____

#276. Understanding Matter & Energy 4

¹ H Hydrogen 1.0079	
³ Li Lithium 6.941	⁴ Be Beryllium 9.012
¹¹ Na Sodium 22.990	¹² Mg Magnesium 24.305

The simplest element is **hydrogen** with an **atomic mass** of 1.00794. Most of that mass resides in the single particle called a proton that forms its **nucleus**. All **protons** carry a positive charge.

1. Hydrogen has an atomic mass slightly larger than _____.

2. Most of hydrogen's mass is in the particle called a _____.

Name: _____ Date: _____

Physical Science

#277. Figuring Out Matter & Energy 1

The **density** of a substance is its **mass per unit volume**. Water has a density of 1 gram/ cm^3 (cm^3 = cubic centimeter). Anything with a density less than 1.0 will float. Oil has a density of 0.93 g/cm^3.

Answer the following questions. If a tanker carrying crude oil sinks and the oil spills:

1. which animals and plants will be most affected? Explain.

   _____

   _____

2. how will the density difference between oil and water make cleanup easier?

   _____

   _____

   _____

#278. Figuring Out Matter & Energy 2

The **boiling point** of a liquid depends on the pressure of air molecules above it (**atmospheric pressure**). When atmospheric pressure is lower, liquids boil at a lower temperature.

Explain why it is impossible for Sammy to get a "really hot" cup of cocoa while camping at 14,000 feet in the mountains:

_____

_____

_____

_____

_____

_____

#279. Figuring Out Matter & Energy 3

Elements are made up of one kind of atom. **Compounds** are molecules made up of more than one kind of atom. **Mixtures** are collections of compounds or elements that don't interact chemically (although one substance might dissolve in another).

Put an "E" next to elements, a "C" next to compounds, and an "M" next to mixtures.

1. gold ring _____   2. sugar water _____

3. table salt _____   4. soft drink _____

5. alcohol _____   6. raisin bread _____

7. water _____   8. iodine _____

9. aluminum tent pole _____

#280. Figuring Out Matter & Energy 4

Discover the mystery element! (You will need to look at a copy of the Periodic Table of the Elements.) Remember, an element's **atomic number** appears in the box with its **chemical symbol** in the table.

Procedure: Add the atomic # of sulfur to the atomic # of uranium. Subtract the atomic # of astatine, and multiply by the atomic # of helium.

What is the mystery element?

_____

Name: _____ Date: _____

Physical Science

#281. Simple Machines 1—Work

Work is a force that causes **displacement**. For example, if you lift a book off a table, work has been performed. Energy has been transferred from you to the book. Draw a diagram to show the transfer of energy for the activities below.

1.
   player $\xrightarrow[\text{energy}]{\text{work}}$ bat $\longrightarrow$ ball

2.
                                              pins

3.   nail

#282. Simple Machines 2—Wedges

A **wedge** is a **simple machine**. It uses a pair of **inclined planes** to make a small force more powerful. An ax is a good example of a wedge.

Circle the wedge in each group.

1. car tire   ax   seesaw
2. front tooth   bike wheel   elevator
3. scooter   snowplow   wheelbarrow
4. doorknob   rubber band   chisel
5. hammer   nail   box
6. backrest   mattress   night stand

#283. Simple Machines 3—Ramps

An **inclined plane**, or **ramp**, is a slope. It increases distance and makes it easier to raise a heavy object from one point to another.

Unscramble the name of each inclined plane.

1. eelcairwhh rmpa

   _____

2. aeewfry omnrap

   _____

3. idbgre cproapah

   _____

4. ovmgin avn oalindg rpam

   _____

5. hisp's gpnglanak

   _____

#284. Simple Machines 4—The Wheel

The **wheel** makes work easier in many ways.

Fill in the missing letters to create a list of devices that include a wheel.

1. F __ __ r __ s wh __ __ l
2. w __ __ __ rw __ __ el
3. st __ __ __ i __ g w __ __ el
4. f __ n
5. s __ in __ __ ng w __ __ __ l

Name: _____ Date: _____

Physical Science

#285. Simple Machines 5— Wheels and Axles

Wheels and axles are found on trains, cars, and trucks. This **simple machine** is also part of countless **complex machines**.

Circle the item that contains a wheel and axle in each set.

1. freeway onramp   doorknob   ax

2. zipper   seesaw   skateboard

3. bike   front tooth   arm

4. backpack with pockets

   purse with clasp

   rolling suitcase

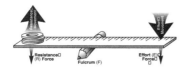

#286. Simple Machines 6—Screws

A **screw** is a useful **simple machine**. If you look at a screw carefully, you will see that it is really a **ramp** spiraling around a central core. The spiral makes the ramp longer, and that makes each part of the work easier.

Find and circle an example of a screw in each line.

1. bulscrspiralstaircasebodrjoin

2. jatyespboltthrpiconnhosew

3. spibocorkscrewjoiyhtrctihs

4. corscrspijarlidthreadralst

5. jatpldhsedrillbitvsebomett

6. bltmmxcflightbulbendrep

#287. Simple Machines 7—Levers

Force or **effort** is applied to one side of the **lever** to lift a **load** or overcome some **resistance** on the other side. The balance point of a lever is called the **fulcrum**.

Circle the items that are NOT levers. Write the items that ARE levers on your own paper.

seesawaxonrampbicyclewheel

bicyclehandbrakeswheelbarrow

bottleopenertoilethandlegardenhoseend

nailclipperstaplerscrewnailarm

noseeartongstweezerscandle

#288. Simple Machines 8—Pulleys

Pulleys use at least one wheel and some rope or chain to make work easier. Use words from the box to complete the paragraph.

distance	load	machine	pulley
pull	energy	raise	force

Have you ever watched someone _____ or lower a flag on a pole? If so, you have seen a _____ in action. A pulley makes it easier to lift a _____. Like the screw, it lowers the amount of effort or _____ needed by increasing _____. For example, you probably noticed how many times the person had to _____ on the rope to raise that flag. He was applying _____ to a simple _____.

Name: _____   Date: _____

Science & Technology

#289. Science & Technology 1

Write the letter of the best word or phrase from the box on each line.

> **A. windmills   B. harness   C. reserves**
> **D. turbine   E. wind farm**

1. Spinning rotor blades in a _____ change steam to electricity.
2. Oil _____ will not last forever.
3. Scientists are working to _____ the power of the wind.

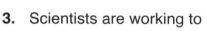

4. On the great plains, farmers used _____ to pump water from wells.
5. A _____ near us uses several windmills to contribute clean energy to the grid.

#290. Science & Technology 2

Circle the best word to match each clue.

1. air resistance:

   lift   airfoil   drag

2. pressure of air pushing a wing up:

   weight   lift   thrust

3. curved shape of the top of a wing:

   thrust   drag   airfoil

4. force experienced because of gravity:

   weight   thrust   lift

5. forward push:

   lift   thrust   airfoil

#291. Science & Technology 3

Unscramble each term associated with nuclear reactions.

1. breaking apart the nucleus of an atom to release energy:

   snsiofi _____

2. giving off energetic particles:

   rdioctaivea _____

3. element used in some nuclear power plants:

   aumnuri _____

4. particle that strikes and breaks apart a nucleus in a chain reaction:

   tonuenr _____

#292. Science & Technology 4

Fill in the missing letters.

1. A network for distributing power is a

   g __ __ d.

2. The electricity delivered to your house is

   a __ t __ __ n __ t __ __ g current.

3. Cables are part of the power

   d __ __ tr __ b __ t __ __ n system.

4. Before arriving at our home, electricity passed through a local

   s __ __ s __ __ t __ __ n.

Name: _____ Date: _____

Science & Technology

#293. Science & Technology 5

Write the letter of the correct word on each line.

| A. telegraph | B. transmit | C. Morse |
| D. Marconi | E. device | |

Samuel (**1**) _____ developed a code for the (**2**) _____, an electrical (**3**) _____ designed to (**4**) _____ messages over a wire. Guglielmo (**5**) _____ is famous for his work on the radio, a way to send information through the air without a wire.

#294. Science & Technology 6

Circle T for true or F for false.

T   F   **1.** **Telecommunication** is another word for a television news report.

T   F   **2.** An **amplifier** makes a signal more powerful.

T   F   **3.** An **antenna** can be used to send or receive radio signals.

T   F   **4.** A **communications satellite** is always located on top of a hill.

T   F   **5.** If a station transmits television signals, it is **broadcasting**.

#295. Science & Technology 7

Fill in the missing letters.

1. Thomas Edison created the first practical **ph** __ __ __ **g** __ __ __ **hic** recordings.

2. A **m** __ **g** __ __ **t** __ **c** recording is stored on a special tape.

3. A **d** __ **g** __ **t** __ **l** recording is read by a laser.

4. The letters in the word **l** __ __ __ **r** stand for light amplification by stimulated emission of radiation.

#296. Science & Technology 8

Circle the best term to fit each clue.

1. information sent:

   signal   modem   decode

2. changes computer data to phone signals:

   vacuum tubes   modem   circuit

3. a set of symbols used to talk to a computer:

   chip   conductor   code

4. using integrated circuits or transistors:

   insulated   electronic   portable

5. to change information into usable form:

   decode   signal   fetch

Name: _____ Date: _____

Science & Technology

#297. Science & Technology 9

Unscramble each term.

1. A clock with a face and hands is an

    laoang _____ device.

2. A clock with numbers that change is a

    giiatdl _____ device.

3. A **itb** _____ can be either 0 or 1.

4. A **teyb** _____ is eight

    sitb _____.

#298. Science & Technology 10

Fill in the missing letters to match each clue.

1. controls the flow of electricity in electronic

    devices: **tra __ __ i __ t __ r**

2. common element used in making

    semiconductors: **s __ l __ c __ n**

3. special chip that performs basic computer

    operations:

    m __ c __ opr __ c __ ss __ r

4. tiny silicon wafer with an integrated circuit:

    c __ __ p

#299. Science & Technology 11

Circle T for true or F for false.

T F **1.** Printers, scanners, and cameras are **peripherals**.

T F **2.** A monitor is a kind of **keyboard**.

T F **3.** A page being printed from the computer is **input**.

T F **4.** A letter being typed into a word processing program is **output**.

#300. Science & Technology 12

Unscramble each term.

1. data:

    iatioronfmn _____

2. a structured collection of information:

    taasabde _____

3. a system of linked computers:

    nerktwo _____

4. directions telling a computer how to

    perform a task:

    rparogm _____

Name: _____ Date: _____

Science & Technology

#301. Science & Technology 13

Fill in the missing letters.

1. the first workable model of a manufactured item:

   p __ __ t __ t __ __ e

2. eye scans and fingerprint keys are examples of:

   b __ __ m __ tr __ __ s

3. making machines very small:

   m __ ni __ t __ ri __ __ t __ __ n

#302. Science & Technology 14

Match each term to the best definition.

____ 1. anything that is man-made or artificial

____ 2. a moldable synthetic material

____ 3. synthetic fabric made from plant material

____ 4. a synthetic fabric made from chemicals

____ 5. a natural fabric made from sheep hair

A. polyester
B. wool
C. plastic
D. rayon
E. synthetic

#303. Science & Technology 15

Unscramble each term.

1. Field biologists track wolves with radio **smrtarsteitn**. _____

2. The **lznidseatniaio** _____ process creates freshwater from salt water.

3. **tnevsanocori** _____ practices help preserve natural resources.

4. Something added to the environment that is harmful to living things is called **oplinoutl**. _____

#304. Science & Technology 16

Fill in the missing letters.

1. Using DNA information to change plants and animals is **g __ n __ t __ c** engineering.

2. **P __ st __ c __ d __ s** kill insects that destroy crops, but they can harm wildlife.

3. **B __ __ l __ g __ c __ l** pest control is a way to protect crops without insecticides.

Name: _____ Date: _____

Science & Technology

#305. Wind Energy & Technology 1

Match the terms to the correct examples. The terms may be used more than once.

> **A. advantage**   **B. disadvantage**

_____ **1.** Wind energy is clean, renewable, and doesn't produce greenhouse gases.

_____ **2.** Wind machines can harm wildlife, such as birds that fly near them.

_____ **3.** Wind speed changes often, and on some days there isn't any wind.

_____ **4.** The source of wind energy is free.

#306. Wind Energy & Technology 2

Match the terms to the correct definitions.

> **A. vertical-axis wind turbine**
> **B. horizontal-axis wind turbine**

_____ **1.** looks like a giant, two-bladed egg beater

_____ **2.** has either two or three blades; looks like a fan

#307. Wind Energy & Technology 3

Different devices are used to measure and harness the wind. Draw a line to connect the wind instrument to its function.

1. anemometer   A. measures wind speed

2. wind vane   B. wind speed scale

3. wind turbine   C. determines wind direction

4. Beaufort Scale   D. converts kinetic energy to electrical energy

#308. Wind Energy & Technology 4

Today, **wind turbines** are being built to provide electrical energy to power homes and businesses. Wind produces **kinetic energy** that turns the blades of a turbine; this drives a generator that produces **electricity**. Electricity travels through a transformer and into local electrical networks through transmission lines that distribute electricity to homes.

1. Wind produces _____ energy.

2. True or False? Wind energy is used to produce electricity. _____

Name: _____ Date: _____

Science & Technology

#309. Solar Energy & Technology 1

Solar panels are devices that can be placed on buildings to absorb and collect **solar radiation** to heat water. The panel is a glass-covered box. A black pipe runs through the box. The black pipe absorbs the sunlight, and the water flowing through the pipe is heated.

Solar panels can be placed on buildings to

_____ and _____

solar radiation to heat water.

#310. Solar Energy & Technology 2

Using solar energy has advantages and disadvantages. Match the terms to the correct examples. The terms may be used more than once.

A. advantage   **B. disadvantage**

_____ **1.** solar technology is expensive

_____ **2.** free, renewable, and clean

_____ **3.** reduces our dependence on foreign sources of energy

_____ **4.** unreliable

#311. Solar Energy & Technology 3

Match the terms on the left to the correct definitions.

_____ **1. inexhaustible**   **A.** heat energy

_____ **2. solar energy**   **B.** unlimited

_____ **3. thermal energy**   **C.** solar cell

_____ **4. photovoltaic**   **D.** solar radiation

#312. Solar Energy & Technology 4

Sunlight is collected by a **photovoltaic** (PV) device or solar cell and transformed into a small amount of electrical energy.

1. True or False? A solar cell can be used to transform radiant energy from the sun into electrical energy. _____

2. A solar cell is also known as a _____ device.

Name: _____ Date: _____

Science & Technology

#313. Geothermal Energy & Technology 1

Match the type of **geothermal power plant** to one of its properties below.

> **A. binary cycle**   **B. flash steam**
> **C. dry steam**

_____ **1.** releases high-pressure hot water from deep reservoirs

_____ **2.** steam only (no water)

_____ **3.** transfers heat from geothermal water to a second liquid

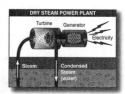

#314. Geothermal Energy & Technology 2

Cirlce the correct answer.

Geothermal energy comes from

A. Earth's sun.

B. tides.

C. dams.

D. Earth's interior.

#315. Geothermal Energy & Technology 3

Which of the following is a disadvantage of **geothermal energy**?

A. Geothermal energy has no **emissions** from burning fuels.

B. Geothermal power plants can only be built in areas where **geothermal reservoirs** are close to the earth's surface.

C. Geothermal energy will never run out.

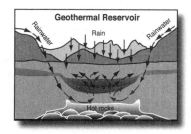

#316. Geothermal Energy & Technology 4

Draw lines to connect the terms on the left to the correct definitions.

1. reservoir   **A.** heat energy stored in the earth

2. thermal   **B.** heat

3. geothermal energy **C.** water storage

Name: _____ Date: _____

Science & Technology

#317. Hydroelectric Energy & Technology 1

Match the terms to the correct examples. The terms may be used more than once.

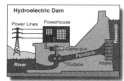

Hydroelectric Dam

> A. advantage
> B. disadvantage

_____ 1. nonpolluting energy source

_____ 2. dams and power stations are expensive

_____ 3. wildlife habitat destroyed by dam building

_____ 4. dams can be built anywhere there is a steady flow of water

#318. Hydroelectric Energy & Technology 2

Connect the terms on the left to the correct examples on the right.

1. **inexhaustible resource**   **A.** water

2. **nonrenewable energy**   **B.** coal

                                        C. petroleum

                                        D. solar energy

#319. Hydroelectric Energy & Technology 3

Hydro energy is used to produce **electricity**. **Hydroelectricity**, also known as **hydropower**, is generated in **hydroelectric power stations**. Some power plants use **dams** to produce electricity, and some do not.

1. True or False? All power plants use dams to generate electricity. _____

2. Hydroelectricity is also known as

_____.

#320. Hydroelectric Energy & Technology 4

Dams are built on rivers and lakes. This creates **reservoirs** where the water is stored. Releasing the stored water through big pipes called **penstocks** causes **turbines** (giant wheels) at the base of the dam to turn. This spins a **generator** that converts the moving water into **electricity**. Electricity is then transported to homes and businesses through power lines.

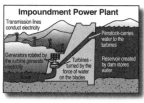

Impoundment Power Plant

1. True or False? Reservoirs are created by building dams. _____

2. True or False? Moving water turns turbines that spin a generator to create electricity.

_____

Name: _____ Date: _____

Science & Technology

#321. Biomass Energy & Technology 1

Biomass is a **renewable** energy source used to produce **biofuel**. Plants and animals used to produce biofuel can be grown over and over. Biomass includes wood and wood wastes, trash from landfill sites, and crop and animal waste. Burning biomass releases the stored chemical energy as heat.

1. _____ is released when

   biofuels are burned.

2. True or False?

   Biofuels such as

   wood and wood wastes are nonrenewable

   energy sources. _____

#322. Biomass Energy & Technology 2

Which is the leading crop used to produce **ethanol** fuel in the United States?

A. soybeans

B. wheat

C. corn

D. beets

#323. Biomass Energy & Technology 3

Match the terms on the left to the correct definitions.

___ 1. **biomass**   A. an alcohol fuel

                       B. a mixture of ethanol

___ 2. **biodiesel**   and gasoline

                       C. plant oil, animal fat,

___ 3. **ethanol**   or grease used as

                            fuel in trucks

___ 4. **gasohol**   D. plant material and

                            animal waste used

                            as fuel

#324. Biomass Energy & Technology 4

Which gas could be responsible for explosions in **landfills**?

A. carbon dioxide

B. ethanol

C. diesel

D. methane

Name: _____ Date: _____

Science & Technology

#325. Nuclear Energy & Technology 1

During the process of **fission**, particles harmful to humans, animals, plants, and the environment are emitted as **radiation**. There is no way to turn **nuclear waste** into something harmless.

1. _____ is emitted during fission.

2. True or False? Nuclear waste is harmless.

    _____

#326. Nuclear Energy & Technology 2

Tell whether each characteristic of using nuclear energy is an advantage or disadvantage. The terms may be used more than once.

A. advantage   B. disadvantage

_____ **1.** expensive to build a nuclear plant

_____ **2.** man-made energy

_____ **3.** produces no carbon dioxide

_____ **4.** concerns about nuclear safety

#327. Nuclear Energy & Technology 3

Nuclear fission takes place inside the **fuel rods**. The energy produced from the nuclear fission heats water in the **core**.

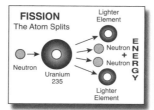

FISSION
The Atom Splits

Neutron

Uranium 235

Lighter Element

Neutron
+
Neutron

E N E R G Y

Lighter Element

The heated water is piped to a machine called a **heat exchanger**. The heat exchanger uses the hot water to boil a huge tank of water to produce steam. The steam is used to generate **electricity**.

1. True or False? Water is heated in the core during fission. _____

2. _____ is generated from steam production.

#328. Nuclear Energy & Technology 4

Match the terms on the left to the correct definitions on the right.

_____ **1. core**

_____ **2. radiation**

_____ **3. uranium**

_____ **4. fission**

A. harmful particles emitted during fission

B. fuel for nuclear power plants

C. splitting atoms of uranium

D. center of a nuclear reactor

Answer Keys

General Science & Inquiry

#001. General Science 1 (p. 2)
1. particle   2. method
3. science   4. expand
5. contract

#002. General Science 2 (p. 2)
1. fact   2. system
3. cause   4. effect

#003. General Science 3 (p. 2)
1. concept, idea
2. observe, watch
3. compare, find similarities
4. contrast, find differences
5. record, write down or save

#004. General Science 4 (p. 2)
1. theory   2. hypothesis
3. experiment   4. identify
5. repeat

#005. General Science 5 (p. 3)
1. state, temporary form
2. force, energy
3. fundamental, basic
4. flow, move
5. unit, part

#006. General Science 6 (p. 3)
1. investigate   2. technique
3. measure   4. condition
5. substance

#007. General Science 7 (p. 3)
1. F   2. T   3. F   4. T
5. F

#008. General Science 8 (p. 3)
1. density   2. speed
3. mass   4. volume
5. weight

#009. General Science 9 (p. 4)
1. True   2. False
3. True   4. False

#010. General Science 10 (p. 4)
1. kilogram, a thousand grams
2. gram, basic metric unit of weight
3. milligram, a thousandth of a gram
4. millimeter, a thousandth of a meter
5. centimeter, a hundredth of a meter

#011. General Science 11 (p. 4)
1. function   2. inference
3. investigate   4. metric
5. model

#012. General Science 12 (p. 4)
1. Venn diagram
2. volume   3. thriving
4. variables   5. transfer

#013. General Science 13 (p. 5)
1. sequence   2. result
3. precise   4. segment
5. name

#014. General Science 14 (p. 5)
1. T   2. F   3. T   4. F
5. F

#015. General Science 15 (p. 5)
1. equilibrium   2. imbalance

#016. General Science 16 (p. 5)
1. collide, run into each other
2. absolute, does not change
3. principles, fundamental rules or laws
4. relative, depends upon changing conditions

#017. General Science 17 (p. 6)
1. scientific law
2. scientific model
3. scientific theory
4. scientific method

#018. General Science 18 (p. 6)
1. T   2. F   3. F   4. T
5. F

#019. General Science 19 (p. 6)
1. frequency
2. interrelationship
3. probable   4. recede
5. advance

#020. General Science 20 (p. 6)
1. replicate, copy
2. submerge, sink
3. boundary, limit
4. inorganic, nonliving
5. significance, importance

#021. Doing Stuff With Matter & Energy 1 (p. 7)
1. The penny tends to stay where it is.
2. Yes   3. friction

#022. Doing Stuff With Matter & Energy 2 (p. 7)
Various answers

#023. Doing Stuff With Matter & Energy 3 (p. 7)
1. volume
2. Put solid in container full of water in a tray, then measure volume of "overflow," which equals volume of solid.

#024. Doing Stuff With Matter & Energy 5 (p. 7)
Various answers, many cleaning compounds

#025–028. Doing Stuff With Living Things: Day 1 Through Day 4 (p. 8)
This set of four activities should be done in sequence. Observations will vary.

#029–032. Doing Stuff With Ecosystems & Habitats: Day 1 Through Day 4 (p. 9)
This set of four activities should be done in sequence. Observations will vary.

#032. Doing Stuff With Ecosystems & Habitats: Day 4 (p. 9)
Make duplicate sets of gardens with controls at room temperature and experimental ones at different temperatures.

#033. Doing Stuff With Astronomy & Space Science 1 (p. 10)
Various answers

#035. Doing Stuff With Astronomy & Space Science 3 (p. 10)
1. Mercury, Venus, Mars, Uranus
2. Neptune

#036. Doing Stuff With Astronomy & Space Science 4 (p. 10)
1. Mars: Phobos
2. Jupiter: Io, Europa, Callisto
3. Saturn: Titan, Mimas, Enceladas
4. Uranus: Miranda

#040. Doing Stuff With Earth Materials 4 (p. 11)
Both artificial and natural rocks are cemented together by process of layering and hydration. In nature, rock formation involves vast time, heat, and pressure.

#041. Doing Stuff With Ancient Life 1 (p. 12)
Problems: May have partial molds and casts; only certain things make impressions; can't tell colors, internal features, etc.

#043. Doing Stuff With Ancient Life 3 (p. 12)
Protection from predators, moisture conservation (for pill bug).

#044. Doing Stuff With Ancient Life 4 (p. 12)
1. C   2. A   3. A   4. B
5. B   6. A   7. B

Life Science

#045. Life Science 1 (p. 13)
1. ecology   2. community
3. biosphere
4. environment
5. adaptation

#046. Life Science 2 (p. 13)
1. classification 2. nonliving
3. organisms   4. species

#047. Life Science 3 (p. 13)
1. carnivores   2. herbivores
3. omnivores

#048. Life Science 4 (p. 13)
1. T   2. F   3. T   4. T
5. F

#049. Life Science 5 (p. 14)
1. mammal, has fur or hair
2. reptile, has scales
3. amphibian, lives part of life on land and part in water
4. bird, has feathers
5. mollusk, is an invertebrate

#050. Life Science 6 (p. 14)
1. calf   2. eye color
3. diving   4. forest
5. kitten

#051. Life Science 7 (p. 14)
1. C   2. A   3. D   4. B

#052. Life Science 8 (p. 14)
1. membrane, a thin wall or layer
2. cytoplasm, contents of a cell, except the nucleus
3. cell, a basic unit of life
4. organelles, tiny structures with special tasks in the cell
5. nucleus, control center of a cell

#053. Life Science 9 (p. 15)
1. F   2. T   3. T   4. F
5. F

#054. Life Science 10 (p. 15)
1. camouflage 2. prey
3. mimicry   4. extinction
5. predator

#055. Life Science 11 (p. 15)
1. branch, crown
2. neither one
3. cone
4. needle, limb

#056. Life Science 12 (p. 15)
1. D   2. A   3. C   4. B
5. E

#057. Life Science 13 (p. 16)
1. photosynthesis   2. leaf
3. oxygen   4. chlorophyll
5. carbon dioxide

#058. Life Science 14 (p. 16)
1. T   2. F   3. T   4. T

#059. Life Science 15 (p. 16)
1. ovary   2. stigma
3. pollen   4. petal
5. pistil

#060. Life Science 16 (p. 16)
1. exchange   2. utility
3. biome   4. physical
5. distribution

#061. Life Science 17 (p. 17)
1. respiration   2. digestion
3. excretion   4. circulation
5. multicellular

#062. Life Science 18 (p. 17)
1. T   2. F   3. T   4. T

#063. Life Science 19 (p. 17)
1. B   2. C   3. A   4. D

#064. Life Science 20 (p. 17)
1. gills, respiratory organ of a fish
2. mates, goose and gander
3. internal, inside
4. external, outside
5. response, reaction

#065. Understanding Living Things 1 (p. 18)
1. producer   2. starch

#066. Understanding Living Things 2 (p. 18)
1. spores   2. gill

#067. Understanding Living Things 3 (p. 18)
1. soil and leaf litter
2. sharpened pencil lead

#068. Understanding Living Things 4 (p. 18)
1. eight
2. front legs, body markings

#069. Figuring Out Living Things 1 (p. 19)
1. a kind of crustacean
2. has 3-part body, 6 legs
3. warm-blooded flyer
4. marsupial mammal
5. has backbone, breathes through skin

#070. Figuring Out Living Things 2 (p. 19)
1. attracts pollinators
2. spores on stalks
3. algae and fungus
4. spores beneath leaves
5. has seeds in cones

#071. Figuring Out Living Things 3 (p. 19)
1. plants   2. protista
3. animals   4. bacteria
5. fungi

#072. Figuring Out Living Things 4 (p. 19)
They confuse the hoods with the surface of a body of water.

#073. Asking About Ecosystems & Habitats 1 (p. 20)
1. Variable, but will probably include E.O. Wilson
2. Variable, could include: Is biodiversity important for a healthy world?

#074. Asking About Ecosystems & Habitats 2 (p. 20)
1. What are examples of insects that live in fresh water?
2. What are a network of food chains in a community?
3. What is the process of change from one community to another?

#075. Asking About Ecosystems & Habitats 3 (p. 20)
1. C   2. D   3. A   4. B

#076. Asking About Ecosystems & Habitats 4 (p. 20)
Is the waste treated? Is the waste dumped upstream of treatment plants? How dangerous is the waste? Many other questions are possible.

#077. Understanding Ecosystems & Habitats 1 (p. 21)
1. False   2. food, pollen

#078. Understanding Ecosystems & Habitats 2 (p. 21)
1. False   2. sea urchins

#079. Understanding Ecosystems & Habitats 3 (p. 21)
1. True   2. family

#080. Understanding Ecosystems & Habitats 4 (p. 21)
1. False
2. food, space, predators

#081. Figuring Out Ecosystems & Habitats 1 (p. 22)
b

#082. Figuring Out Ecosystems & Habitats 2 (p. 22)
They all try to attract pollinators.

#083. Figuring Out Ecosystems & Habitats 3 (p. 22)
Chemicals traveled from the sage to the tobacco on the wind.

#084. Figuring Out Ecosystems & Habitats 4 (p. 22)
Protection, nest, cocoon, etc. Various answers for testing.

Human Body

#085. Human Body 1 (p. 23)
1. cycle   2. organ
3. tissue   4. organ system

#086. Human Body 2 (p. 23)
1. central nervous system
2. brain   3. nerves
4. spinal cord 5. stimulus

#087. Human Body 3 (p. 23)
1. C   2. B   3. A   4. E
5. D

#088. Human Body 4 (p. 23)
1. digestive   2. stomach
3. intestines   4. esophagus
5. liver

#089. Human Body 5 (p. 24)
1. B   2. D/A   3. A/D
4. C

#090. Human Body 6 (p. 24)
1. legs   2. hips
3. knee   4. chest
5. chest

#091. Human Body 7 (p. 24)
1. D   2. B   3. E   4. C
5. A

#092. Human Body 8 (p. 24)
1. optic   2. auditory
3. dentin   4. saliva
5. retina

#093. Human Body 9 (p. 25)
1. gland   2. endocrine
3. adrenal 4. pancreas

#094. Human Body 10 (p. 25)
1. excretory 2. kidney
3. bladder   4. skin
5. urethra

#095. Human Body 11 (p. 25)
1. F   2. T   3. F   4. F
5. T

#096. Human Body 12 (p. 25)
1. D   2. C   3. A   4. B

#097. Human Body 13 (p. 26)
1. T   2. F   3. T   4. T
5. F

#098. Human Body 14 (p. 26)
1. enamel   2. dentin
3. root   4. crown
5. gums

#099. Human Body 15 (p. 26)
1. gene   2. chromosome
3. DNA   4. molecule
5. heredity

#100. Human Body 16 (p. 26)
1. B   2. A   3. D   4. C

#101. Human Body 17 (p. 27)
1. fitness   2. flexibility
3. aerobic   4. endurance

#102. Human Body 18 (p. 27)
1. A   2. E   3. C   4. B
5. D

#103. Human Body 19 (p. 27)
1. retina   2. lens
3. iris   4. pupil
5. cornea

#104. Human Body 20 (p. 27)
2. sweet   3. sour
4. salty   5. bitter
Listed foods will vary.

#105. Observing the Organization of the Human Body 1 (p. 28)
Pulse will be higher standing than sitting and higher running than standing. Pulse results from the beating of your heart.

#106. Observing the Organization of the Human Body 2 (p. 28)
By focusing at a distance, the images from right and left eyes don't merge completely, but partially overlap instead.

#107. Observing the Organization of the Human Body 3 (p. 28)
Incisors cut and shear like scissors. Canines puncture and tear. Molars crush food.

#108. Observing the Organization of the Human Body 4 (p. 28)
1. The right forearm feels cooler.

2. The alcohol evaporates faster, carrying more heat away.
3. Alcohol baths were used to reduce fevers.

#109. Asking About the Organization of the Human Body 1 (p. 29)
1. E/C/D   2. D   3. C

#110. Asking About the Organization of the Human Body 2 (p. 29)
1. immune system
2. respiratory system
3. digestive system
4. skeletal system

#111. Asking About the Organization of the Human Body 3 (p. 29)
1. What are the four major human blood groups/types?
2. What blood cells play a role in the defense of the body?
3. Which chambers of the heart pump blood?

#112. Asking About the Organization of the Human Body 4 (p. 29)
Variable responses.

#113. Understanding the Organization of the Human Body 1 (p. 30)
1. F
2. viruses, bacteria, fungi, insects

#114. Understanding the Organization of the Human Body 2 (p. 30)
1. T   2. contract

#115. Understanding the Organization of the Human Body 3 (p. 30)
1. stroke   2. aneurysm

#116. Understanding the Organization of the Human Body 4 (p. 30)
1. cerebrum, cerebellum, medulla
2. central nervous system

#117. Figuring Out the Organization of the Human Body 1 (p. 31)
a nephron

#118. Figuring Out the Organization of the Human Body 2 (p. 31)
1. D   2. C   3. A   4. E
5. B

#119. Figuring Out the Organization of the Human Body 3 (p. 31)
You will be more susceptible to infection, will show a low white blood cell count, and have a weakened immune system.

#120. Figuring Out the Organization of the Human Body 4 (p. 31)
1. NI   2. NI   3. I   4. I
5. NI

Earth Science

#121. Earth Science 1 (p. 32)
1. crust   2. inner core
3. mantle   4. outer core

#122. Earth Science 2 (p. 32)
1. fault   2. earthquake
3. wave   4. seismograph

#123. Earth Science 3 (p. 32)
1. seismology, study of earthquakes
2. shallow, near the surface
3. tsunami, ocean wave caused by an earthquake
4. tremor, shaking
5. magnitude, size

#124. Earth Science 4 (p. 32)
1. volcanic   2. ash
3. basalt   4. pumice
5. obsidian

#125. Earth Science 5 (p. 33)
1. C   2. D   3. B   4. E
5. A

#126. Earth Science 6 (p. 33)
1. toxic   2. explosive
3. solidify   4. eruption

#127. Earth Science 7 (p. 33)
1. sandstone, sand
2. conglomerate; pebbles, sand, and clay
3. shale, clay
4. limestone, dissolved shells

#128. Earth Science 8 (p. 33)
1. strata   2. erosion
3. weathering
4. conservation
5. resistant

#129. Earth Science 9 (p. 34)
1. luster   2. hardness
3. color   4. streak color
5. crystal shape

#130. Earth Science 10 (p. 34)
1. renewable resource, forests
2. nonrenewable resource, oil
3. alternative energy source, wind energy
4. pollution, smog

#131. Earth Science 11 (p. 34)
1. anthracite   2. bituminous
3. fossils

#132. Earth Science 12
1. C   2. D   3. B   4. A

#133. Earth Science 13 (p. 35)
1. A   2. C   3. B   4. D

#134. Earth Science 14 (p. 35)
1. iceberg   2. retreating
3. advancing   4. valley
5. ice sheet

#135. Earth Science 15 (p. 35)
1. D   2. A   3. E   4. B
5. C

#136. Earth Science 16 (p. 35)
1. current   2. depth
3. salinity   4. marine

#137. Earth Science 17 (p. 36)
1. trenches   2. shallow
3. surface   4. island
5. hot spot

#138. Earth Science 18 (p. 36)
1. crevasse   2. compact
3. debris   4. boulders

#139. Earth Science 19 (p. 36)
1. F   2. T   3. F   4. T
5. T

#140. Earth Science 20 (p. 36)
1. C   2. E   3. D   4. A
5. B

#141. Understanding Earth Materials 1 (p. 37)
1. jagged   2. conchoidal

#142. Understanding Earth Materials 2 (p. 37)
1. Mesozoic
2. old, middle, new

#143. Understanding Earth Materials 3 (p. 37)
1. techtonic plates   2. False

#144. Understanding Earth Materials 4 (p. 37)
1. anticline   2. fault

#145. Figuring Out Earth Materials 1 (p. 38)
Mica

#146. Figuring Out Earth Materials 2 (p. 38)
Quartz

#147. Figuring Out Earth Materials 3 (p. 38)
Hornblende

#148. Figuring Out Earth Materials 4 (p. 38)
Granite

#149. Finding Out About Earth Materials 1 (p. 39)
a. 4 (1815)
b. 1 (1912)
c. 5 (130 B.C.E.)
d. 3 (1842)
e. 2 (1883)

#150. Finding Out About Earth Materials 2 (p. 39)
Arthur Lakes

#151. Finding Out About Earth Materials 3 (p. 39)
1. hard shiny coal
2. base rock under sediments
3. surface above point of origin of earthquake
4. Paleozoic supercontinent

#152. Finding Out About Earth Materials 4 (p. 39)
1. All are dating methods.
2. Radiocarbon dating is most accurate for a 10,000-year-old mammoth.

#153. Observing Ancient Life 1 (p. 40)
1. B   2. D   3. C   4. A

#154. Observing Ancient Life 2 (p. 40)
1 C   2. A   3. B

#155. Observing Ancient Life 3 (p. 40)
C

#156. Observing Ancient Life 4 (p. 40)
1. D   2. A   3. B   4. C

#157. Asking About Ancient Life 1 (p. 41)
1. What are examples of prehistoric sea animals?
2. What are ways to become fossilized?
3. What are the three eras of geological time?

#158. Asking About Ancient Life 2 (p. 41)
1. C   2. B   3. A

#159. Asking About Ancient Life 3 (p. 41)
Variable answers. See if bones are jumbled or articulated. See if bones are oriented in one direction. Look for tooth marks in bone; see if they match allosaur teeth. Check what other kinds of fossils appear.

#160. Asking About Ancient Life 4 (p. 41)
1. B   2. A   3. D   4. C

#161. Understanding Ancient Life 1 (p. 42)
1. False   2. True

#162. Understanding Ancient Life 2 (p. 42)
1. mummify (or dry out), fossilized
2. Charles Sternberg

#163. Understanding Ancient Life 3 (p. 42)
1. False   2. 90%

#164. Understanding Ancient Life 4 (p. 42)
1. river, lake, or ocean
2. minerals

#165. Figuring Out Ancient Life 1 (p. 43)
short-faced bear

#166. Figuring Out Ancient Life 2 (p. 43)
Tyrannosaurus rex

#167. Figuring Out Ancient Life 3 (p. 43)
coelophysis
Image of Coelophysis from: http:commons.wikimedia.org/wiki/File:Coelophysis_mount_NHM2.jpg {{GFDL–Self}} Ballista, photographer

#168. Figuring Out Ancient Life 4 (p. 43)
pteranodon (or pterosaurs)

Atmospheric Science

#169. Atmospheric Science 1 (p. 44)
1. T   2. F   3. T   4. T
5. F

#170. Atmospheric Science 2 (p. 44)
1. anemometer, wind speed
2. barometer, air pressure
3. hygrometer, humidity
4. thermometer, temperature
5. rain gauge, precipitation

#171. Atmospheric Science 3 (p. 44)
1. drought   2. global warming
3. ozone   4. pollution
5. global

#172. Atmospheric Science 4 (p. 44)
1. El Niño   2. cold front
3. warm front
4. transpiration
5. evaporation

#173. Atmospheric Science 5 (p. 45)
1. F   2. T   3. T   4. F
5. F

#174. Atmospheric Science 6 (p. 45)
1. infrared   2. variations
3. carbon   4. circulate

#175. Atmospheric Science 7 (p. 45)
1. cirrus   2. cumulus
3. stratus   4. altocumulus
5. nimbus

#176. Atmospheric Science 8 (p. 45)
1. precipitation 2. pattern
3. hail   4. snow
5. rain

#177. The Atmosphere 1 (p. 46)
Answers will vary. Possible answers inclue: The atmosphere is the layer of air that surrounds the earth and goes up 600 to 6,000 miles (depending on variations in the exosphere). It is made up of nitrogen, oxygen, water vapor, and other gases.

#178. The Atmosphere 2 (p. 46)
1. T   2. T   3. T   4. T
5. F

#179. The Atmosphere 3 (p. 46)
1. nitrogen   2. oxygen
3. water vapor
4. carbon dioxide
5. other gases   6. dust

#180. The Atmosphere 4 (p. 46)
1. 3   2. 1   3. 4   4. 2
Thermosphere should be circled.

#181. The Atmosphere 5 (p. 47)
Weather, heats, unevenly, move, rotation, wind

#182. The Atmosphere 6 (p. 47)
Change *farthest from* to *nearest to*, *meters* to *miles*, *meteors* to *weather*, *increases* to *decreases*, and *tropostop* to *tropopause*.

#183. The Atmosphere 7 (p. 47)
1. troposphere
2. ionosphere
3. stratosphere
4. mesosphere

#184. The Atmosphere 8 (p. 47)
stratosphere

#185. Air Pressure 1 (p. 48)
Gravity, earth, weight, pressure, amount, temperature

#186. Air Pressure 2 (p. 48)
1. No   2. Yes
3. Yes   4. Yes

#187. Air Pressure 3 (p. 48)
1. A beach at sea level
2. The equator
3. A cold, snowy day
4. The stratosphere

#188. Air Pressure 4 (p. 48)
1. cold, good   2. warm, bad

#189. Heat 1 (p. 49)
1. C   2. B   3. A

#190. Heat 2 (p. 49)
1. T   2. T   3. F   4. T

#191. Heat 3 (p. 49)
Sunlight strikes the equator at an angle close to 0 degrees. It is more efficient, brighter, and warmer. Near the poles, the sunlight strikes at nearly a 90-degree angle. It doesn't warm very efficiently, making temperatures colder.

#192. Heat 4 (p. 49)
molecules, dense, slow, sinks, rise, movement

#193. Winds 1 (p. 50)
1. air pressure 2. high, low
3. heating

#194. Winds 2 (p. 50)
Anemometer

#195. Winds 3 (p. 50)
1. coming from
2. from, to
3. higher, lower

#196. Winds 4 (p. 50)
1. The Doldrums
2. Trade winds
3. Polar Easterlies
4. Prevailing Westerlies

#197. Water in the Atmosphere 1 (p. 51)
1. water vapor
2. rain, sleet
3. snow, hail, frost

#198. Water in the Atmosphere 2 (p. 51)
1. B   2. D   3. A   4. C

#199. Water in the Atmosphere 3 (p. 51)
1. oceans   2. puddles
3. leaves   4. streams
5. ponds   6. seas
7. soil   8. lakes

#200. Water in the Atmosphere 4 (p. 51)
less, water vapor, liquid, crystals, condensation, atmosphere

#201. Water in the Atmosphere 5 (p. 52)
1. C   2. B   3. A   4. D

#202. Water in the Atmosphere 6 (p. 52)

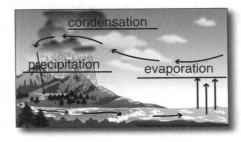

#203. Water in the Atmosphere 7 (p. 52)
1. C   2. D   3. A   4. B

#204. Water in the Atmosphere 8 (p. 52)
1. cumulonimbus   2. cirrus
3. stratus
4. nimbo- or nimbus

#205. Precipitation 1 (p. 53)
Any form of water that falls from the clouds and reaches the earth's surface. Examples: rain, snow, sleet, hail, freezing rain (any three)

#206. Precipitation 2 (p. 53)
1. T   2. F   3. F   4. T
5. F

#207. Precipitation 3 (p. 53)
1. E   2. D   3. A   4. B
5. C

#208. Precipitation 4 (p. 53)
1. rain
2. They reflect light.
3. a rain gauge

#209. Air Masses & Fronts 1 (p. 54)
pressure, temperature, humidity, million

#210. Air Masses & Fronts 2 (p. 54)
1. air pressure
2. temperature
3. wind direction
4. moisture

#211. Air Masses & Fronts 3 (p. 54)
1. tropical: forms over the tropics;
   warm
2. polar: forms north or south of 50-degree latitudes; cold
3. maritime: forms over oceans; humid
4. continental: forms over land; dry

#212. Air Masses & Fronts 4 (p. 54)
1. T   2. T   3. T   4. F

#213. Air Masses & Fronts 5 (p. 55)
1. Yes   2. Yes   3. No
4. Yes

#214. Air Masses & Fronts 6 (p. 55)
1. slowly   2. cirrus
3. snow

#215. Air Masses & Fronts 7 (p. 55)
1. stationary front
2. extended wet and cloudy weather

#216. Air Masses & Fronts 8 (p. 55)
1. AC   2. C

#217. Storms 1 (p. 56)
1. cumulonimbus   2. rises
3. heavy

#218. Storms 2 (p. 56)
lightning

#219. Storms 3 (p. 56)
1. twister
2. waterspout
3. dust devil

#220. Storms 4 (p. 56)
1. 370 mph
2. a few minutes
3. Water is heavier than air.

#221. Storms 5 (p. 57)
1. T   2. T   3. F   4. T

#222. Storms 6 (p. 57)
1. C   2. B   3. A

#223. Storms 7 (p. 57)
hurricane, tropical, winds, low, spinning, land

#224. Storms 8 (p. 57)
1. lower, faster
2. lowest, warmest, center

Space Science

#225. Space Science 1 (p. 58)
1. asteroid   2. comet
3. meteor   4. meteorite

#226. Space Science 2 (p. 58)
1. constellation 2. galaxy
3. star   4. black hole

#227. Space Science 3 (p. 58)
1. inner planets   2. orbit
3. outer planets   4. planet

#228. Space Science 4 (p. 58)
1. inner planets   2. rocky
3. Mercury   4. Venus
5. Earth   6. Mars

#229. Space Science 5 (p. 59)
1. outer   2. gaseous
3. Jupiter   4. Saturn
5. Uranus   6. Neptune

#230. Space Science 6 (p. 59)
1. Milky Way   2. telescope
3. cluster   4. local group
5. nebula

#231. Space Science 7 (p. 59)
1. D   2. C   3. A   4. B

#232. Space Science 8 (p. 59)
1. pulsar   2. red giant
3. supernova 4. quasar

#233. Space Science 9 (p. 60)
1. sunspots   2. flare
3. corona   4. eclipse
5. ultraviolet

#234. Space Science 10 (p. 60)
1. D   2. A   3. B   4. E
5. C

#235. Space Science 11 (p. 60)
1. dwarf
2. Kuiper belt
3. asteroid belt
4. impact
5. bodies

#236. Space Science 12 (p. 60)
1. C   2. A   3. D   4. E
5. B

#237. Asking About Astronomy & Space Science 1 (p. 61)
1. Jupiter   2. Saturn
3. Mars   4. Venus

#238. Asking About Astronomy & Space Science 2 (p. 61)
1. B   2. C   3. A   4. D

#239. Asking About Astronomy & Space Science 3 (p. 61)
Variable answers

#240. Asking About Astronomy & Space Science 4 (p. 61)
1. B   2. D   3. A   4. C

#241. Understanding Astronomy & Space Science 1 (p. 62)
1. seven
2. average, yellow

#242. Understanding Astronomy & Space Science 2 (p. 62)
1. False   2. True

#243. Understanding Astronomy & Space Science 3 (p. 62)
1. rings   2. 1997

#244. Understanding Astronomy & Space Science 4 (p. 62)
1. sunspots   2. Galileo

#245. Figuring Out Astronomy & Space Science 1 (p. 63)
Some things would have no use on the spacecraft and be forgotten; a crew in close quarters would need motivation to go on the trip and be able to work with each other for their entire lifetimes.

#246. Figuring Out Astronomy & Space Science 2 (p. 63)
The riverbeds were present after the period of cratering.

#247. Figuring Out Astronomy & Space Science 3 (p. 63)
Earth moves slower than Venus in its orbit, but faster than Mars. When Earth overtakes Mars, Mars appears to slow and back up before going forward again.

#248. Figuring Out Astronomy & Space Science 4 (p. 63)
The nearer objects move against the star field.

Physical Science

#249. Physical Science 1 (p. 64)
1. spectrum   2. infrared
3. ultraviolet 4. rainbow
5. optics

#250. Physical Science 2 (p. 64)
1. technology   2. fiber
3. metal   4. nonmetal
5. gold

#251. Physical Science 3 (p. 64)
1. concave   2. convex
3. absorption   4. refraction
5. reflection

#252. Physical Science 4 (p. 64)
1. enlarge, magnify
2. instrument to see faraway things, telescope
3. instrument to see very small things, microscope
4. instrument with two enlarging lenses, binoculars
5. glass curved to bend light, lens

#253. Physical Science 5 (p. 65)
1. F   2. T   3. F   4. T
5. F   6. F

#254. Physical Science 6 (p. 65)
1. oscillate   2. amplitude
3. repetition   4. frequency

#255. Physical Science 7 (p. 65)
1. metal   2. melted
3. nonmetal   4. metallurgist
5. alloy

#256. Physical Science 8 (p. 65)
1., 2., 4., and 5. should be circled.

#257. Physical Science 9 (p. 66)
1. component   2. compound
3. mixture   4. solution
5. suspension

#258. Physical Science 10 (p. 66)
1. gas   2. liquid
3. solid   4. melt
5. solidify

#259. Physical Science 11 (p. 66)
1. atom   2. molecule
3. element
4. periodic table
5. properties

#260. Physical Science 12 (p. 66)
1. attract   2. repel
3. compass   4. positive
5. negative

#261. Physical Science 13 (p. 67)
1. B   2. A   3. D   4. C
5. E

#262. Physical Science 14 (p. 67)
1. C   2. D   3. B   4. A

#263. Physical Science 15 (p. 67)
1. circuit   2. breaker
3. insulator

#264. Physical Science 16 (p. 67)
1. accelerate   2. decelerate
3. velocity   4. momentum

#265. Physical Science 17 (p. 68)
1. kinetic   2. stationary
3. conversion   4. potential

#266. Physical Science 18 (p. 68)
1. waste   2. destroyed
3. Heat   4. Hydroelectricity

#267. Physical Science 19 (p. 68)
1. transfer energy   2. create
3. replaceable
4. supplemental

#268. Physical Science 20 (p. 68)
1. C   2. D   3. A   4. E
5. B

#269. Observing Matter & Energy 1 (p. 69)
Variable answers

#270. Observing Matter & Energy 2 (p. 69)
1. liquid   2. solid
3. liquid   4. gas
5. liquid   6. solid
7. gas   8. liquid

#271. Observing Matter & Energy 3 (p. 69)
Variable answers

#272. Observing Matter & Energy 4 (p. 69)
A. 3   B. 2   C. 5   D. 4
E. 1

#273. Understanding Matter & Energy 1 (p. 70)
1. inertia
2. grams or kilograms
3. matter

#274. Understanding Matter & Energy 2 (p. 70)
1. elements   2. compound

#275. Understanding Matter & Energy 3 (p. 70)
1. similar
2. the Periodic Table of the Elements

#276. Understanding Matter & Energy 4 (p. 70)
1. 1   2. proton

#277. Figuring Out Matter & Energy 1 (p. 71)
1. The ones that live on shore or near the surface of the water will be most affected, because the oil will float.
2. It should be possible to skim the oil off the top of the water.

#278. Figuring Out Matter & Energy 2 (p. 71)
Air pressure is less, so water boils at a lower temperature.

#279. Figuring Out Matter & Energy 3 (p. 71)
1. M (The gold would likely not be pure in a ring.)
2. M   3. C   4. M   5. C
6. M   7. C   8. E   9. E

#280. Figuring Out Matter & Energy 4 (p. 71)
Palladium (atomic #46)

#281. Simple Machines 1— Work (p. 72)
2. bowler $\xrightarrow{\text{work}}$ ball $\xrightarrow{\text{energy}}$ pins

3. worker $\xrightarrow{\text{work}}$ hammer $\xrightarrow{\text{energy}}$ nail

#282. Simple Machines 2— Wedges (p. 72)
1. ax
2. front tooth
3. snowplow
4. chisel
5. nail
6. backrest

#283. Simple Machines 3— Ramps (p. 72)
1. wheelchair ramp
2. freeway on-ramp
3. bridge approach
4. moving van loading ramp
5. ship's gangplank

#284. Simple Machines 4— The Wheel (p. 72)
1. Ferris wheel
2. waterwheel
3. steering wheel
4. fan
5. spinning wheel

#285. Simple Machines 5— Wheels and Axles (p. 73)
1. doorknob
2. skateboard
3. bike
4. rolling suitcase

#286. Simple Machines 6— Screws (p. 73)
1. spiral staircase
2. bolt
3. corkscrew
4. jar lid thread
5. drill bit
6. lightbulb end

#287. Simple Machines 7— Levers (p. 73)
Not Levers: ax, on-ramp, bicycle wheel, garden hose end, screw, nail, nose, ear, candle
Levers (in any order): seesaw, bicycle hand brakes, wheelbarrow, bottle opener, toilet handle, nail clipper, stapler, arm, tongs, tweezers

#288. Simple Machines 8— Pulleys (p. 73)
raise, pulley, load, energy, distance, pull, force, machine

Science & Technology

#289. Science & Technology 1 (p. 74)
1. D   2. C   3. B   4. A
5. E

#290. Science & Technology 2 (p. 74)
1. drag
2. lift
3. airfoil
4. weight
5. thrust

#291. Science & Technology 3 (p. 74)
1. fission
2. radioactive
3. uranium
4. neutron

#292. Science & Technology 4 (p. 74)
1. grid
2. alternating
3. distribution
5. substation

#293. Science & Technology 5 (p. 75)
1. C   2. A   3. E   4. B
5. D

#294. Science & Technology 6 (p. 75)
1. F   2. T   3. T   4. F
5. T

#295. Science & Technology 7 (p. 75)
1. phonographic
2. magnetic
3. digital
4. laser

#296. Science & Technology 8 (p. 75)
1. signal
2. modem
3. code
4. electronic
5. decode

#297. Science & Technology 9 (p. 76)
1. analog
2. digital
3. bit
4. byte, bits

#298. Science & Technology 10 (p. 76)
1. transistor
2. silicon
3. microprocessor
4. chip

#299. Science & Technology 11 (p. 76)
1. T   2. F   3. F   4. F

#300. Science & Technology 12 (p. 76)
1. information
2. database
3. network
4. program

#301. Science & Technology 13 (p. 77)
1. prototype
2. biometrics
3. miniaturization

#302. Science & Technology 14 (p. 77)
1. E   2. C   3. D   4. A
5. B

#303. Science & Technology 15 (p. 77)
1. transmitters
2. desalinization
3. conservation
4. pollution

#304. Science & Technology 16 (p. 77)
1. genetic
2. Pesticides
3. Biological

#305. Wind Energy & Technology 1 (p. 78)
1. A   2. B   3. B   4. A

#306. Wind Energy & Technology 2 (p. 78)
1. A   2. B

#307. Wind Energy & Technology 3 (p. 78)
1. A   2. C   3. D   4. B

#308. Wind Energy & Technology 4 (p. 78)
1. kinetic
2. True

#309. Solar Energy & Technology 1 (p. 79)
absorb, collect

#310. Solar Energy & Technology 2 (p. 79)
1. B   2. A   3. A   4. B

#311. Solar Energy & Technology 3 (p. 79)
1. B   2. D   3. A   4. C

#312. Solar Energy & Technology 4 (p. 79)
1. True   2. photovoltaic

#313. Geothermal Energy & Technology 1 (p. 80)
1. B   2. C   3. A

#314. Geothermal Energy & Technology 2 (p. 80)
D

#315. Geothermal Energy & Technology 3 (p. 80)
B

#316. Geothermal Energy & Technology 4 (p. 80)
1. C   2. B   3. A

#317. Hydroelectric Energy & Technology 1 (p. 81)
1. A   2. B   3. B   4. A

#318. Hydroelectric Energy & Technology 2 (p. 81)
1. A, D   2. B, C

#319. Hydroelectric Energy & Technology 3 (p. 81)
1. False   2. hydropower

#320. Hydroelectric Energy & Technology 4 (p. 81)
1. True   2. True

#321. Biomass Energy & Technology 1 (p. 82)
1. Heat   2. False

#322. Biomass Energy & Technology 2 (p. 82)
C

#323. Biomass Energy & Technology 3 (p. 82)
1. D   2. C   3. A   4. B

#324. Biomass Energy & Technology 4 (p. 82)
D

#325. Nuclear Energy & Technology 1 (p. 83)
1. Radiation   2. False

#326. Nuclear Energy & Technology 2 (p. 83)
1. B   2. A   3. A   4. B

#327. Nuclear Energy & Technology 3 (p. 83)
1. True   2. Electricity

#328. Nuclear Energy & Technology 4 (p. 83)
1. D   2. A   3. B   4. C